Grief
to
Generosity

Grief to Generosity
Honor Your Child by Helping Others

Cover design by Andrew Hudson
Handprint art by E.Speshneva/Shutterstock.com

Interior Book Design and Layout by
www.integrativeink.com

ISBN: 978-0-578-40110-2

Grief
to
Generosity

Honor your Child
by Helping Others

A Guide By
Peggy Oliver Krist

About the Cover

An early memory of leaving our mark as children is a clay handprint that we give our parents. Like the prehistoric cave dwellers, we symbolically mark our spot with our hand. Things haven't changed in 40,000 years. As humans we still need to cry out, "I was here, don't forget me."

DEDICATION

To you, the reader.
Although we are joined in tragic loss,
we also have in common our need
to keep our child present in our lives.

CONTENTS

Preface

Grief to Generosity
Honor Your Child by Helping Others

You have suffered an unthinkable loss: the death of your child. I hope my book can serve as a roadmap for you as you pull out of spiraling grief and move into something positive.

This book is a set of lessons to help you navigate the obstacles you'll face if you choose to publicly memorialize your child. It is a resource I wish I'd had at the beginning of my journey, when I had no idea how to deal with our son's death or how to honor his memory. This is how I found my way back: I kept my heart and mind together and did the work our son didn't finish.

When your child's tribute takes root through giving, your child feels present. But it's a slow and bumpy process. The 10 steps to philanthropy listed in my book are meant to lead you beyond your grief. As you start to get involved with your mission, you need to be aware of how your grief still follows you and disrupts you. The 10 common challenges illustrate some of the unique issues familiar to all bereaved parents working in philanthropy. I share what we faced in our outreach—and I hope that our stories will prepare and inspire you.

At least 40,000 books have been written about grief and dealing with the loss of a child, and more than 8,500 books about philanthropy. I gained some great insights from the books I read, but none of them actually described the nuanced journey from grief to philanthropy. The books focused on one subject or the other, but I couldn't compartmentalize the process that way—it's not how I experienced it. So I wrote my book to share my experience with you.

My husband and I lost our youngest son, Jonathan, in 2006. Though only 19, Jonathan was a very talented musician and a committed social activist. We stumbled into the non-profit sector when a family friend and lawyer suggested we establish a public foundation to help guide us through our grief. I wasn't prepared to find my responsibility so emotionally charged. We were given a chance to pass Jonathan's future on to those less fortunate, and we do. But from day one it's been a blessing and a curse.

Mourning takes work. When I got a grip on the process, I realized that our outreach wasn't just about memorializing our son by helping others as he had done. It was also about helping other parents deal with the death of a child by channeling their despair into action.

I'd like to think my real job is to pay it forward, to help guide you in your journey as you bid your child a final goodbye.

*Handling change
is like jumping into a deep river.
You better learn to go with the flow
or you'll never reach higher ground.*

—Kabrien Goss, 6th grade student
Foundation Academies, Trenton, NJ

Grief

We have in common the loss of a loved one.
In the next few pages
I'll share our son's death with you.
His name is Jonathan,
but sometimes we call him Jonny.

In the rest of the book I describe the lessons
we learned when we stepped
into the world of philanthropy in his name.

That work helped our family heal,
but in telling our story to you
I have tried to keep my mourning present,
because it was.

ON HIS WAY HOME

O ut of death came life. That night, and my memory of the night he died, was the beginning of my journey from grief to generosity. I just didn't know it at the time.

Wednesday, May 31, 2006. 1:00 a.m. What I remember most is that I feared the worst. Jonathan wasn't home yet, even though he was due to leave that morning to hike the Appalachian Trail with his older brother Matthew. Something was wrong. Nervous, I went out to look for him in the middle of the night. I couldn't find him anywhere.

2:10 a.m. I returned home, frightened by the unknown.

2:38 a.m. I hadn't thought to drive to Bowman's Hill Wildflower Preserve, a 134-acre park that borders our town in Bucks County. That's where Officer Koretzky found him—just north on River Road, alone, in the red Hyundai Sonata with the roof caved in.

4:19 a.m. Officer Koretzky approached our front door in the dark, accompanied by two uniformed policemen and a man in green scrubs. I heard the rap of firm knuckles on the door. My husband woke from his half slumber. Together, knowing the truth before we knew the facts, Bob and I opened the door.

4:25 a.m. All four men had the somber look of having done this before, waking parents to tragedy in the middle of the night. Officer Jonathan Koretzky, a towering six foot six, calmly delivered what police call "the notification."

"Jonathan was on his way home. He was in a very serious traffic accident on River Road. He suffered major injuries and died at the scene." Silence. "He died at the scene." Dead.

At that very moment we both recognized "the end,"—the "nothing will ever be the same in our lives" end. We were at the zero point. Our spirits were permanently reset to zero and the rest of our lives divided in two; the life before Jonathan died and the life after.

5:15 a.m. Officer Koretzky drove us to Doylestown Hospital. I remember not crying. When we arrived at the morgue, Deputy Coroner Preston repeated the details of the accident. Even with our son's 19-year-old corpse laid out in front of us, I asked the coroner over and over again, in disbelief: Why? Why did his dear heart stop? Where was the blood? And again. Why wasn't there any blood? Why wasn't his nose broken? Did he feel it? What music was he listening to before he crashed? He's a musician, there must have been music! What is adrenaline? And again. Why did his big, generous heart stop beating? When?

I touched Jonny's quiet heart. My tears finally gathered.

A plain white sheet was folded neatly across his chest. His face was quiet, eyes closed. The remains of life still lingered. I felt his bony fingers, with the creased grooves left by the strings of his upright bass. I expected a broken nose or a battered face, but all I saw was the old scar on his right brow from the time he slipped on the ice in Pisgah Forest a few years back.

I bent down to lay my cheek on his, expecting the scent of salty sweat from when he was playing Frisbee the afternoon before. Instead I smelled the leftover coroner fixings in his hair. I felt the last unresolved struggle in him put to rest on that hospital gurney, that last day of May.

I came to regret not spending more time with Jonny as he lay in the morgue, silent, like a discarded cocoon. But I didn't have the perspective to know then what I know now. Jonathan was slowly becoming something different to me. He was becoming an old soul.

6:10 a.m. I thought I would faint in the elevator. Instead, I kept asking Officer Koretzky, who so far had guided us through every blinding turn, what his name was. When he told me his first name was Jonathan, I squeezed his hand and responded, as if to politely acknowledge that I'd just encountered a ghost, "That's my dead son's name. He's left us. Did you know him?"

Of course he didn't *know* our son. No one involved in Jonny's last moments on earth *knew* him. They just guided him through. In the years to follow, all the people we'd meet in his memory wouldn't *know* him. But it didn't matter. The only way out of our sorrow was through.

6:45 a.m. Officer Koretzky drove us back from the hospital, patiently listening to us weep in the backseat, where he usually transported misfits and criminals. We had no idea where we were going, let alone where we'd just been. Maybe I'd dreamed all this stuff, I thought. Maybe Jonathan had come home while we were away.

Unlike the last moments of Jonathan's life, on *our* lonely ride home, I felt trapped, yet completely shielded from danger. I wanted to scream, but I couldn't. I just sat upright in a stupor, handcuffed in shock to Bob.

Two days later, Jonathan looked a lot different. Richard McDonough, the mortician, had taken him to his funeral home and prepared him for others. When I first saw him in his casket, I waited for him to raise his eyebrow, give me that familiar wink and tell me this was all a big joke. There was no response. I waited, but Jonathan didn't have a mark of rebellion or rhythm left in him.

On that Friday, hundreds of people lined up outside the funeral home in the rain, loyal family and friends came to pay their respects and take witness of the unthinkable: young Jonathan Krist was dead.

The Zero Point

When Jonathan died, our spirits were permanently damaged. The rest of our life divided in two: the life before he died and the life after. Grieving parents call this defining moment in loss "the zero point." The precise boundary in our family history is May 31st, 2006, 2:38 a.m.

At the time we lived in a restored mill on Ingham Creek in New Hope, Pennsylvania. I watched our three sons—Matthew, Brian and Jonathan—grow up there, and I expected them to grow old together. Sometimes I imagined them married and living here with lots of kids. In my daydreams they still looked like teenagers, just older and with less hair, playing their guitars on the side porch and scaring off the deer in the backyard.

Bob is a professional photographer, and he and I worked together in his career, traveling the globe in many roles for *National Geographic*. We led an interesting and charmed life. Life was good, really good. Then Jonathan died and our lives changed.

When we began the process of recovering from his death, we knew we had to do more than bury him: we needed to figure out how to keep him present. At first, I tried to do that by spending hours in his room, laying out his old clothes and music. Then we tackled some of the unfinished projects Jonathan himself had embarked on before his death.

We could have supported music programs and cleaned up wetlands in his memory without a formal entity. Our family decided a lasting legacy should take on a legal form. Eventually we awkwardly plowed through paperwork in the office of our lawyer, a family friend, learning how to establish the Jonathan D. Krist Foundation. Years passed until we understood the impact of this decision and the positive effect it had on our family and the people we help.

In the chapters that follow you'll learn more about the projects we undertook in Jonny's memory. All of these efforts were guided by my maternal instinct telling me I must do something to make our situation better. While I couldn't change the outcome, I could set a course for our sons Matthew and Brian.

My response to Jonathan's death began in darkness. In the beginning there was no room for grey, or even light. But I had to *choose* to do something, even if only for the sake of his brothers. They helped me see the need to move toward the light. They became my anchor in grief.

You will need someone to help you set anchor, too.

ABOUT JONATHAN

Jonathan was an activist and freshman at Oberlin College. A talented musician, he was politically conscious, aware even at a young age that he'd been born into the right zip code. He'd start a political discussion around the dinner table, or lead a formal debate at his school about labor unions. Often, he responded to an issue by taking action—collecting band instruments for a rural charter school in North Carolina, for example, and raising funds to build wells in Africa.

Knowing that, it was easy for us to decide where to start with our outreach—right where Jonathan had left off. Jonathan had gathered instruments that had been lying around unused at friends' houses, politely rescuing them from dusty attics and hall closets. He'd been planning to donate them to the KIPP charter school, Gaston College Prep, that he'd learned about when his oldest brother was considering teaching there. I took the band instruments to North Carolina.

As for those wells in Africa: We hadn't known about Jonathan's fundraising until we found a poster tucked among his band music. The poster was for a campaign he'd started in 2004 as student body president at his high school. We learned that the money would go to an organization called PlayPumps International in Africa. (The PlayPump is an ingenious solution to providing schools with clean drinking water. It's basically a merry-go-round attached to a conventional borehole pump, and when children spin it around, using it for playground fun, they're pumping water to an above-ground tank.) We decided to raise the money to build that well in Malawi.

And so we began our outreach, in a very grassroots way—because that was Jonathan's style. He was a bit of a contrarian with a wicked sense of humor; he didn't always play by the rules. We tried to follow suit. The small lessons we learned through our first forays into the field humbled both of us, but especially me, and were to guide us in our future work.

ABOUT THE ZERO POINT

In the first few months after Jonny's death, doing charitable deeds in his name helped our family rise from the zero point. I stepped into the lives of so many strangers who needed help, and I tried my best to assist them. Some of their needs were bigger than me, and I learned that I had to set boundaries. But I did what I could, and every bit of help I gave also helped me to heal. Essentially, I took from every person I met.

At times, the spirit of our son loomed large. Jonny had an uncanny ability to make people grin, while at the same time drawing them into an uncomfortable political discussion. I felt him lingering in every grateful handshake from someone he would never know. Those first efforts made Jonathan feel present to me, so I accepted that direction: to step in and help, one person at a time.

But then the next wave of grief would hit us. And when it did, we four gathered and retreated to our home, a home that no longer had Jonathan in it.

"*You think it begins to diminish with time, the pain, then it comes back and hits you with a rawness and freshness you had forgotten.*"

— William Boyd
Any Human Heart

THE BLESSING AND THE CURSE

As I've said, countless books have been written on the process of mourning. Many of these books guide parents through what's become known as the Kubler-Ross five stages of grief: denial, anger, bargaining, depression, and acceptance. Most days you will cry so hard you'll think your eyes have been permanently damaged. You'll feel the loss of your child so deep in your bones you'll have no idea what stage of grief you're in, nor will you care.

And then there are all the emotions you'll feel inbetween those accepted stages of grief, emotions that will leave you totally detached, sometimes for months—or even, in my case, for years. You'll be gripped by things like fear, confusion and hope; by the relentless sympathy of others, the indifference, and the excuses people make for fate; by alcohol, guilt and fears for your health; by the religious explanations and by black humor. But eventually you will reach the stage of forgiveness, and then you will just long for the life you had before your child died.

Through it all, I managed to keep Jonny present. And I'm still holding on, because I learned that our outreach in Jonny's name could mean that I'd never have to let go of his memory. Whenever someone held out a "faith card," I ignored it. Grief doesn't denote a lack of faith, nor does hope particularly indicate the presence of it. Instead, I decided to play the "hope card," because I was determined to remain optimistic.

And the longer I held on to Jonathan, the more good things started to happen to me. Strangers I would never have met entered my life. I found myself in places previously unknown to me, such as a part of eastern North Carolina that's plagued by generations of poverty. Our family went from the gritty backstreets of Camden, New Jersey, to the homes of the Washington DC elite, attending a PlayPumps International reception hosted by Steve Case, the founder of AOL and a philanthropic supporter of water rights.

With each new encounter I was forced to deal with the best and worst emotions Jonny's death had left in me. In all these places I was welcomed, and found no room for self-pity.

But for quite a while, I remained in the anger stage of grief. I couldn't find a therapist who'd lost a child, so I never saw one. The truth is, I didn't trust my sorrow with anyone but my husband. No parent should outlive their children, and I still resent not having the chance to say goodbye to our son. I don't need a professional to point out that nearly 12 years later, I'm still not willing to let go of his death.

That's the curse.

But as our middle son, Brian, has so keenly observed, our foundation allows me to still be a mother to Jonathan. This is how I heal. I simply hang on to our son in his "afterlife" and carry out the work he'd be doing if he were still alive.

We are grateful for the people who lent us their support. After Jonathan's memorial service his grandparents offered to help a local student in his memory. Friends and family gave money in his name. Others volunteered. More checks and donations piled up at his high school. And the donations continue to this day.

That's how money gets tangled in with love. People from church, or from your child's chess club, soccer team or place of work, will want to help. It's human nature. Most banks honor checks for six months, so in the beginning you can put them away in an envelope while you take time to think about your plan.

So many people refused to let us forget the intentions of our caring, social-activist son. One of these was our friend and lawyer, Peter Reiss, who encouraged us to establish a foundation. In Step Ten I will share some of the questions we discussed with him.

At the end of the first year we mailed out our first annual letter with Jonny's new last name on it: "Foundation." That's when I realized I had moved into the best stage of grief: the gift of time.

That's the blessing.

*"Where there is much light,
The shadows are deepest."*

—Johann Wolfgang von Goethe
Author and statesman, 1749–1832

Paying It Forward

Since my teen years I've written short essays and kept journals, recording the stuff of life with no regard for an audience. I wrote every day after Jonathan died, and organized my mourning into a book for my immediate family. It was more of a personal timeline of our grief, like the scrapbooks that keep us from forgetting our family's precious memories.

This book is not a sad memoir. *Grief to Generosity* is meant to be a handbook, a trusted guide in the darkness. It's one of the ways I'm paying it forward, since I know I can't give Jonathan's future back to him. I hope it will help the next bereaved mother deal with that awful epiphany. That's what my friend Penny Meier did for me—she helped me adapt from grief to generosity.

Penny was the first person who spoke honestly to me about losing a child. In 1990 she and her husband had lost their college-age daughter, Stephanie, to an illness. In our first year of mourning, I confided to Penny that the blissful curiosity that had once governed our lives was gone. Bob and I continued to meet our obligations, but the real joy of life had abandoned us. Her advice came as a welcome relief.

"Don't expect to recover from Jonathan's death," Penny told me. "All you need to know is that you won't always feel as bad as you do now. You'll develop a public persona that will help you move forward." She was right.

On the outside my wound may have looked repaired, as if the doctor had removed the stitches and I was fixed. The truth is that I'd buried the pain deep enough in my body so it didn't rupture in public. The remedy I learned from Penny is that there *was* no remedy for my sorrow. There was no "Get Out of Jail Free" card, so I stopped expecting one.

By year three I had found the public persona Penny described, but I was still seeking the same quiet resolve I saw in her. For me, grief hasn't been a linear experience; it shows up unexpectedly. I long for the assurance I took for granted as a young mother—tucking my baby boy in after a bedtime story, knowing he'd wake in the morning.

And now, in year 12, I have found some clarity in my grief. I want to share how we created our lasting tribute to our son. I am not an expert. Like you, I am searching for a remedy. If my book inspires just one bereaved parent to take action, I will have paid it forward.

MEETING GINNY

I met Ginny Riedley through our mutual lawyer about three years into my mourning. Ginny had lost her daughter Tara, an accomplished lawyer and equestrian, in 2008. Just 30 years old, Tara died in her sleep from heart problems during a family vacation in Cancun.

Now it was my turn to pay it forward; to share with Ginny the problems we'd faced when we started our outreach.

Ginny had several questions about the non-profit process. Despite being sad and overwhelmed, she, too, was trying to lead her family into something positive. The problem was that she and her husband Roger couldn't move in sync: When Ginny was ready to commit to an athletics event, he had gone into grief freeze. When he was ready to award their first scholarship, Ginny couldn't get out of bed. It sounded all too familiar to me.

But like us, they bravely moved forward. They suspected that taking action would mute their grief, and so it did. Meeting with Ginny was like holding a mirror up to myself. That's when I knew that eventually, I would have to write this book. But it was still too early for me to start.

(And just as I had supported Ginny when she started a charity of her own, about eight years later Ginny would help me write down an ending for mine. She taught me that every family should prepare an exit strategy for their work. I wasn't ready to do that until—well, until I wrote this book. Oddly enough, the end is something you need to think about, even right at the beginning.)

What I didn't understand then, but know now, is the value of waiting. When Jonathan died, our lives shattered like a 1,500-piece jigsaw puzzle dumped in a pile on our living room floor. The work we did in Jonny's memory put some of the puzzle back together, but it took years for us to make sense of the bigger picture and learn what our foundation could become.

I gained perspective on our loss from the insightful writings of German theologian Dietrich Bonhoeffer. He explained that God kept the "gap"—Jonathan's absence—empty, so we can still feel our son's presence. Over time I started connecting the small yet significant acts that happened in those empty gaps. As I made the connections, our outreach took on new meaning.

> *"Nothing can make up for the absence of someone whom we love, and it would be wrong to try to find a substitute; we must simply hold out and see it through. That sounds very hard at first, but at the same time it is a great consolation, for the gap, as long as it remains unfilled, preserves the bonds between us.*
>
> *It is nonsense to say that God fills the gap; God doesn't fill it, but on the contrary, keeps it empty and so helps us to keep alive our former communion with each other, even at the cost of pain."*

—Dietrich Bonhoeffer
Theologian and martyr, 1906–1945

STRENGTHENING THE BOND

When significant moments began happening, I thought for a while that they were random. With time, I realized they were connections that, even in death, were meant to be. Here's an example: In 2008, with the generous help of

18

music producer Ian Kelly, we delivered a 15-piece Yamaha drum set to a music class at Trenton Central High School in New Jersey. Ian, who also lives in New Hope, had wanted to replace the worn drums at Trenton High. (Some of the bass drum heads were held together with Band-Aids.) He had the connections at Yamaha to make this happen; he just needed a charitable organization, like ours, to get it done.

After the students unpacked the new drums, they invited us to stand with them, hand in hand, in their prayer circle. Gratefully, we joined in. As the year passed, Ian kept returning to Trenton High to help at band practices, bringing in professional musicians like Gerald Heyward and Pablo Batista. Our son Brian filmed the school's drumline performing at parades and football games in Trenton.

And after we talked to the music students about water rights and the PlayPump well in Africa, the drumline decided to pay it forward. They raised money for PlayPumps by performing first at a student assembly for our high school in New Hope, and then at a basketball game in our school's gym. It felt like Jonathan was present. The pieces came together and filled the empty gap, right there on the basketball court where Jonny used to shoot hoops.

Another example of connections being forged: In 2010, we watched a door open between Camden, New Jersey, and Oberlin, the elite private college in the Midwest where Jonathan had been a student.

Through our foundation we'd become involved with two inner-city schools in New Jersey. We produced our own video about water rights and the PlayPump well to show at a fundraising event around World Water Day. The noted author James McBride, a friend of Ian's, agreed to participate in the video. When I asked James how I could repay him, he suggested I contact the band teacher at Creative Arts high school in Camden, New Jersey. I did so the next day, and learned that the jazz program needed instruments. That's how I ended up in Camden in 2009. I bought new and used instruments and drove them to South Sixth Street.

The first student I met there, Alex Cummings, would later become the first student from Camden to be admitted to Oberlin Conservatory.

The next year, Kirk Norris, a Quaker activist from New Hope, introduced me to Foundation Academies, a Trenton charter school where orchestra is required of every student. I started arranging for students from both schools to perform together and to attend a summer music camp we had organized, Jazz Academy at Solebury School.

As it turned out, the Dean of Oberlin Conservatory learned of our outreach from three of his faculty members who volunteered at our Jazz Academy program. I know that college football coaches recruit, but I didn't think conservatory deans did that, so I was impressed when Dean Stull showed up at these two New Jersey high schools to support the one discipline many American schools have abandoned: music.

Dean Stull later told us that he'd been inspired by our outreach and used it as a model to create his Music In America program. Besides visiting these schools in search of musical talent, he also brought the schools' music teachers to the Oberlin campus to inspire his college graduates to commit to careers in teaching.

And by 2017, several Camden students had graduated from Ohio's Oberlin College. It gave me hope.

Not only did the puzzle begin to come together, but so did the serendipity: it kept on occurring, making our outreach more and more meaningful. And so I learned to remain open to new ideas and to cultivate our grassroots approach.

When these connections develop in your outreach, you'll know what to do. You will start paying it forward, and that will fill the emptiness.

Step in. It's addictive.

Any outreach is good for you. It can be a simple act of kindness: Say, you could fill a basket for a heart patient with lotions, a book, slippers and a robe. Or you could anonymously pay off the lunch bill for a school that needs support. But if you're thinking about a larger commitment, like a formal charity in your child's name, remember to keep it simple. Really, any gesture keeps the relationship with your child going.

Vernon Brim was one of the students in that prayer circle at Trenton High. After watching the PlayPumps video, he made an astute comment that humbled me and put my loss into perspective. "We have our troubles in Trenton," he said, "but unlike the kids in Africa, at least we have shoes on our feet."

You too have to be grateful for something.

If you held your child before his last breath, be grateful.

If your child experienced joy and friendship in his lifetime, be grateful.

If you have other children beside you now, be very grateful.

Compassionate Friends

"There are no strangers here—only friends you have not yet met."

—William Butler Yeats
Irish poet, 1865–1939

Don't be afraid to seek out other bereaved parents. They understand.

During our lives, we all belong to different clubs. I was always in a parent-teacher club. For a while I was in a tennis club. About six months after Jonathan died I reluctantly attended a few meetings of The Compassionate Friends, an organization made up of bereaved parents. I was welcomed unconditionally. Unless you're in this club, you won't understand why we don't mind having a good cry with complete strangers.

After a year or so, our friends had stopped mentioning Jonny's name in conversations. In these meetings with strangers, I learned to always ask a grieving parent for the name of their child. I also learned to say my own dead child's name out loud and often. I learned how to include our son in our future by talking out loud about Jonathan's life. Try to do the same, weaving a memory of your child into everyday conversations whenever you can.

The Compassionate Friends has been supporting bereaved families for more than four decades through a network of some 660 chapters. It began when a chaplain in England brought together two sets of grieving parents, and realized that the support they gave each other was better than anything he could provide as a chaplain. The group adopted the butterfly as its logo, symbolizing the renewal of life. Elizabeth Kubler-Ross writes about seeing drawings of butterflies on the walls of children's dormitories in World War II concentration camps—perhaps a sign that the children knew their fate and were leaving a message.

It has taken some humility on my part, but now, whenever a butterfly is in sight, I accept that our son has emerged into a more graceful and free existence. And that's a gift, because it's a reminder to let go of my obsession with his death. (I'm still working on the forgiveness thing.)

The Compassionate Friends supports families in many ways. Whatever the cause of your loss, whatever your circumstances, they are available to help. You can learn more and find the location of the closest chapter at compassionatefriends.org.

I tremble with gratitude
*   for my children*
*   and their children*
who take pleasure in one another.

*   In our dinners together,*
*   the dead enter*
*   and pass among us*
*   in living love and in memory.*

*   And so the young are taught.*

—Wendell Berry
Author, Leavings 1934–

Generosity

"The magic of the human soul

is the more

it gives

the more it's whole."

—John Beacher
Songwriter

INTRODUCTION
TEN STEPS TO GENEROSITY

There's no right or wrong way to grieve or to pay it forward.

This book is meant to help other families who choose to find their way out of grief by memorializing their child in a public tribute. This can take the form of volunteering with a local charity, creating your own non-profit, managing an annual event, or simply planting a tree, or observing a day of silence.

It was important for our family to keep Jonathan present by doing something for others. Like us, you should just begin, however awkward and heavy you feel. Your spirit is broken, but in time you will learn how to repair it.

Start by getting outside, if only to breathe different air. Rise up, get out of the house and move forward instead of dwelling on the way things used to be. That place only gets darker.

Remember, the work you will be doing is not about you. Let your child's spirit be your guide. When I walked in Jonathan's shoes, our mission statement and objectives followed, as did the money—and our friends.

Keep your plan simple and uncomplicated, but expect a landslide of good will and good intentions. However, don't let it consume you.

That's my general advice. What follows in this section is a description of the 10 practical, positive steps that guided us into philanthropy and at the same time defined the boundaries of my sorrow. I hope they can lead you into a positive place as well.

Step One: Shield Yourself

Mourning takes work, especially in public. Prepare yourself.

The dialogue of grief is always awkward, so you need to be prepared. One way to do that is by memorizing a stock response to protect yourself from friends and neighbors inquiring after your well-being. My response was, "Thank you. I appreciate your concern, but I'm late for an appointment." It would stop the conversation in its tracks—and help me avoid a meltdown.

Find a few public hiding places where you can escape from your neighbors. Because eventually you have to get out of the house, and grief will creep in when you least expect it—say, when you're grocery shopping. I hid in the detergent aisle, where I could let the tears roll down. No one else ever hangs out in the detergent aisle.

Another trick I learned: Imagine that a window shade is pulled down in front of you. You can see out, but no one can see in. During those first few months of sorrow, that's how I insulated myself in public: whenever I left the house, I pulled down my window shade.

The only phrases a grieving parent wants to hear is something along the lines of "I miss your child, too" or

"Can I bring dinner over tomorrow?" Not so welcome are the phrases I started to hear after a few months, things like "move on" and "let go," even from well-meaning friends and family. Some even asked why our son had been driving so fast, a question that caused a lump in my throat every time. In those instances, my memorized response provided a graceful end to the conversation.

Mourning takes time. Give yourself time to mend.

To further shield yourself in public, define boundaries to separate your philanthropic goals from your private life. Maintain your strength by taking a lot of naps. No cause is worth becoming a stranger to your family and friends, or to yourself.

There is no right or wrong way to mend. There is only time. Time will nourish you.

STEP TWO: TAKE NOTES

Always have a small journal and a pen or pencil handy to write down your thoughts. You have to teach yourself to think differently, and writing will help you navigate this process of change.

Writing through Mourning

After Jonathan died I took notes, dutifully recording the tidal wave of emotions that swept through our family in the summer of 2006. If you think it's hard to find missing car keys after age 50, it's even harder to find a purpose in life when you've lost a child. So I took notes. And I buried my musings, the way a secret drinker hides a bottle, in my dresser drawer under the fancy silk scarves that had once been my mother's.

Letters to my dead son started in a small, worn journal that followed me everywhere. I jotted notes on flimsy white bar napkins and the backs of old envelopes. I stuffed index cards in my pocket so I could record any ideas that came to me, whether I was on a bike ride or waiting in line at the post office. Write down all your thoughts.

My journal was a private refuge, a way to conceal what I didn't dare confide. Taking notes made me think. Thinking made me retrace Jonny's last steps. And retracing his accident on paper was less stressful than unloading on my family.

In one year my body felt 10 years older and oddly disfigured by his death. My posture was crooked; I was disoriented. In solitude, I waited out the pain and my haunted thoughts. My journal was the only place where I could safely question my sanity.

During that first year I always carried an index card inscribed with four sentences I'd written to introduce myself in public. I was incapable of memorizing this text, so the card kept me from meandering into incoherent conversations with strangers. It read:

"Jonathan was an activist and freshman at Oberlin College. He died in a car accident the night before he was to hike the Appalachian Trail. As a student leader he worked on two causes: building wells in Africa and collecting band instruments for underserved schools. And that's why I'm here, to finish what he started."

When I asked a friend to suggest some books that might guide me through my grief, he told me that the next book I should read was the book I needed to write. And so, before I could forget everything, I wrote *On His Way Home: A Tribute to Jonny*. Self-published in 2010, it was filled with personal family memories and what I'd learned, at the time, about death and my stages of grief. You will forget so many details later, so remember them now—and write them down.

To help establish a routine for your journal, write a letter to your child once a year. Choose the same day—perhaps her birthday, the anniversary of her death, or the day she would be voting. This annual reckoning will become a sort of subterranean current that pulls you back into your personal, quiet memorial. The writing prevents you from drowning.

To stay motivated, enroll in a writing class. This is when I honed some of the technical skills of the craft and also learned to focus. When I was in my depths of grief I just wanted to go howl at the moon. But when I expressed my feelings in my journal, I moved forward, word by word. In class I also met people who, like me, were navigating through mourning and writing about loss.

That habit of taking notes carried over into our outreach. I always have a notebook on hand when I meet with non-profit leaders, environmentalists and teachers. I keep binders to hold the photos, newspaper clippings and notices of the events we've sponsored. I record every donation and every investment in others to remind me of Jonathan.

You won't regret saving your journals, along with any correspondence you receive, big or small. For years, I kept all the sympathy cards we received, tucking them into one of Jonny's scuffed guitar cases.

"Never forget that writing is as close as we get to keeping a hold on the thousand and one things— childhood, certainties, cities, doubts, dreams, instants, phrases, parents, love—that go on slipping, like sand, through our fingers."

— Salman Rushdie
British Indian novelist, 1947-

Step Three: Start Small

It's natural to think that small acts of kindness won't make a difference, but they do.

Do anything that feels relevant in your child's name. Sign up for a work weekend at Habitat for Humanity, or run in a Race for the Cure. When you can't sleep at night, cook with reckless abandon and take the dishes to your community food bank. Collect books for an under-resourced library; perhaps that will lead you to build a memorial reading garden in your child's memory.

What you have in common with every bereaved parent is your child's funeral. Send a donation to The Unforgettables Foundation and help low income families give their children a dignified burial. Start with one person, one meaningful gift at a time, and see where it goes.

The Jonny Scholars

One very generous, unconditional act marked the beginning of Jonathan's foundation. A few days after the memorial service at our high school, we encountered Jonny's grandfather, Harold Krist, standing mutely in the driveway between our homes. It was clear that he hadn't slept. Exhausted and lost for words, he hugged us and held out a check for $5,000, going through the quiet motions of deliberate giving.

Jonathan was fortunate that his paternal grandparents, who met in England during WWII, lived right next door. During high school he'd visit on Tuesday nights to cook pop-overs and play cards. He heard about the wartime dances in Plymouth, England, and the often-told story about the time his grandfather was mistaken for a teletype repair-man, which delayed his landing until several days after the D-Day invasion.

By 2006, Jonathan's grandmother had suffered at least two mini-strokes, and she was in bed when her three children gathered to tell her the news of Jonny's accident. Joyce laid back on her pillows, gasping for air and repeat-ing "Jonny, Jonny, Jonny." Perhaps she was recalling his last visit with her, on her birthday, when they played cards at her dining table and he came from behind to win a game of Casino. But now she looked and sounded like a ghost, faintly calling his name.

Several days later, my sister-in-law Carol helped her mother prepare to go to the funeral home, combing Joyce's thinning hair and tying a box of tissues to the arm of her wheelchair. After Harold put on his only dark suit, now a size too big, Carol maneuvered her parents to the wake. I'll never forget their stunned, waxen stares. They sat by Jonny's coffin like statues, survivors of World War II, and bravely watched their oldest son bury his youngest child. Sadly, Joyce would be dead a year later.

In 2012, some of the students who received awards show where they added their names on the Jonny signature guitar.

When Jonathan's grandfather handed us that $5,000 gift, it was a week before New Hope Solebury High School's graduation in 2006. We decided to give the money to Jade Greene, who was graduating and needed financial help for college. Jade and Jonathan had worked together at the school on environmental issues, and on the final day of his life, she was the last person to see Jonny and me together.

We hadn't yet established our foundation, but that award, our first formal act in Jonny's name, would eventually expand into our scholarship program, The Jonny Scholars. Little did I know that our first scholar would still be involved with our family today. In time, Jade became part of our World Water Day event, promoting water rights and raising money for the PlayPump well in Africa. She would also be back on stage at New Hope Solebury High School in 2016, to present that same scholarship to Jake Dupont.

By June 2018, we had recognized 46 students as Jonny Scholars. All of them have benefitted from the college experience. Yes, two or three dropped out, but they didn't "drop down". I keep tabs on those students because they questioned everything from the start. One is still figuring it out and the other two, after a long pause, eventually transferred to colleges that were a better fit. Looking back, and with a graduation rate of nearly 98%, I think the odds are in our favor to bank on equal access to education.

> *"No one could make a greater mistake than he who did nothing because he could only do a little."*
>
> — Edmund Burke
> British statesman, 1729–1797

Take notes.

Take inventory.

Take courage.

Step Four: Take Inventory

Even if you've already launched a few small volunteer projects, at some point you should sit down and list your skill sets. That will help you figure out what you're good at and what you're willing to do. For instance, I'm good at managing money but a bit overwhelmed by screen time, so my husband handles social media. Are you a good organizer, event planner, or greeter? Can you handle a budget? Perhaps you enjoy construction, or tutoring, or making a meal for fifty.

Or are you willing to shave your head for a cause? Ethan Toohey and Robert Nagg were two New Hope-Solebury students whose lives were tragically cut short from cancer. In 2017 more than 80 supporters in their community shaved their heads to raise money in the boys' memory, bringing in more than $74,000 for St. Baldrick's, a private funder of childhood cancer research grants.

And consider the inspiring story of Alex Scott in Manchester, Connecticut. Alex was only four when she started a lemonade stand to raise money for childhood cancer research. A fighter, she'd been battling cancer since her diagnosis while she was still a baby. Her example inspired others around the country to start similar fundraisers.

Though Alex died at age eight in 2004, the Alex's Lemonade Stand Foundation is still going strong, and has raised more than $150 million for the cause.

The Box of New Hope

After awarding our first scholarship in June 2006, we took stock of our skills. In 2002 Bob had published a coffee-table book on Bucks County, with many photos of our hometown. We got the idea of raising funds by creating notecards that we'd call the Box of New Hope.

Bob and I felt comfortable about taking this project out into the public. It would help keep our son's aura alive through photography—the medium we know best. We had the know-how, and a network of contacts, to put the idea to work. Our school community needed to be part of a positive project in Jonny's memory, too. And I had to get myself out of our lonely house and back to a familiar place, like our school. Our plan was that money raised from the sales would pay for bigger "boxes of hope" that we'd give to people in need.

Volunteers helped print and package the cards, and students from New Hope Solebury's business club stepped up to sell them. The kids also helped stuff boxes with useful items like blankets and bus passes, filled want lists for soldiers at Walter Reed Hospital, and dropped off canned goods at our local food pantry and the Rescue Mission in Trenton. We donated money to make a home in New Hope wheelchair-accessible for two children who suffer from SMA syndrome. We shipped used books to schools. We sent cameras to the Goodlands Project in northeast Philadelphia, which empowers young people to focus on the positive aspects of their neighborhood through photography. And, of course, we delivered band instruments to places where they were needed.

After Hurricane Katrina hit Louisiana, a year before Jonny died, he voiced his concerns for the people who had been displaced, and pictured their personal belongings, like horns and violins, floating about in the Gulf marshes. Because of our memories of Jonny's post-Katrina empathy, we decided that our first instrument delivery would be to New Orleans. It was the place that had nurtured Louis Armstrong, Buddy Bolden, Irvin Mayfield and Wynton Marsalis, and Jonathan's life had been totally wrapped up in their music. (A dear friend once called Jonny "an old jazzman at heart.") We learned that the legendary jazz club Tipitina's had started "Instruments A-Comin" to help school music programs after the hurricane, so we shipped their volunteers a donated amp, a guitar, a couple of horns and a box of music supplies.

Ideas for new projects kept coming. Jonathan had repaired bikes, so along with some student volunteers we partnered with New Hope Cyclery and over three years collected 170 used bikes to donate to Pedals for Progress. This charity provides economic aid to the developing world by sending them used bikes and sewing machines. Students in our community who ride bikes for recreation quickly learned that in the third world, bikes are for basic transportation—but are also put to use as taxis, trash haulers and produce carriers.

In the business club meetings at New Hope Solebury, I tried to encourage students to see beyond the doom and gloom they expressed about the world. My theme was "Response is what matters." I must have been channeling Jonny when I found myself saying, "Your business club doesn't have to be about the business of money. Think about a cause you're passionate about and use your business skills to support a social solution." I suggested they compare our country now to the way it was after the Civil War. "No matter how bad the world gets, civilization always leans toward hope," I told them. "You can too, especially if you know what you're really passionate about."

Well, I'd like to think I convinced at least one business student to consider working in philanthropy rather than taking a job on Wall Street. I do know that I gave them a hitching post for their sorrow. Just as I had learned from working in the Box of New Hope program, they learned that you don't heal from the loss of a loved one because time passes; you heal because of what you do with the time.

JONNY'S SIGNATURE GUITAR

When Jonathan was about 11 or 12, we took him to the Guitar Center in the nearby town of Langhorne because he was itching to play a Paul Reed Smith Custom 24 guitar. The salesman played a Hendrix lick on the expensive model himself, then reluctantly handed it to Jonny. To the salesman's surprise, Jonny ripped into Rimsky Korsakov's "Flight of the Bumble Bee" as a small audience formed around him. The salesman got a small reality check when Jonny politely handed the black guitar back to him saying, "It's not my color!"

Knowing how much Jonny had loved playing Paul Reed Smith guitars, Matthew contacted the company. They invited us to tour their Maryland factory and donated three guitars to our Box of New Hope program. We kept one—a shiny red model called the SE Soapbar—so we'd never forget their kind response. We were still stumbling in our roles back then, but they gave us validation that we were on the right track.

At the first group meeting with our Jonny Scholars in 2007, each college student signed that red guitar. The signatures have since become a tradition, and the guitar will always be a reminder of what nourished Jonny: music. Play it, yes; donate it, no. We could never give that guitar away.

"Nature was his teacher.
Music was his voice."

STEP FIVE: GET OUT OF THE HOUSE

*"Perhaps home is not a place
but simply an irrevocable condition."*
—James Baldwin
Author, 1924–1987

The Road Trip

For some time, Jonathan had been collecting band instruments and supplies for a KIPP charter school in rural North Carolina. KIPP stands for the Knowledge Is Power Program, which runs more than 200 tuition-free public charter schools around the United States. Jonathan had learned about the school's music program when his brother Matthew had looked into teaching there. Okay, so maybe he was also planning the trip as an excuse to cut school and go boogie-boarding on the Outer Banks, but he did have the stuff all boxed up in our garage, ready to go.

That was my direction to move forward: where Jonathan had left off in life. I had band instruments to deliver.

So I loaded up the car, left our uncommonly quiet home where I was feeling smothered by grief, and headed to Gaston, in northeastern North Carolina. At home I kept running into walls, stuck in rooms where I couldn't find the door out. It felt good to be experiencing new territory, and I knew it would distract me.

The moment I arrived at Gaston College Prep, I was inspired. A group of girls were singing "Amazing Grace" in the hallway, and when I heard them I cried. When students in the cafeteria shouted their school chant, I cheered along with them. And when I sat in a quiet classroom and listened to senior Chevon Boone read her poem about choosing not to be ordinary, I believed her.

We tend to live in separate places. According to demographic expert Bert Sperling, the average violent crime rate in the United States is about 30 on a scale of 1–100. In Gaston, the violent crime rate is at least double that. The truth is, random violence and drug abuse respect no boundaries. Certainly parents weren't planning for a funeral when they dropped off their young children at Connecticut's Sandy Hook Elementary School that December morning in 2012. Neither were the mothers of parishioners who were shot dead in historic Emanuel African Methodist Episcopal Church in Charleston in 2015. In my community, four mothers got that devastating call in 2017, when a simple marijuana deal went bad and took the lives of their sons.

Weapons have no boundaries in America anymore, but poverty does. And I crossed that boundary when I drove into Gaston back in 2007. I found myself in a "fly-over zone," a term the school's principal used to describe communities that few people visit. There may be productive farmland and a beautiful lake in the surrounding countryside, but more than 20 percent of people in Gaston live below the poverty line. And until someone steps up, the cycle continues.

Two former Teach for America candidates, Tammi Sutton and Caleb Dolan, did step up. In 2001 these dedicated leaders built a KIPP charter school, Gaston College Prep, at the edge of town on a former peanut farm. Their dream of a quality education became a reality that has since spread to nearby Halifax. Led by a tireless staff of committed educators, KIPP students are redefining the notion of what's possible in public education.

After my first meeting with Gaston College Prep's band director, Kenneth Woodley, I wanted to support his music program. I knew exactly who to call for help. When Jonathan was a high school junior, he'd visited the University of Richmond, in Virginia, and attended an exciting jazz class there led by professor Mike Davison. During that trip Jonny also had the opportunity to perform alongside college music majors.

So in early 2008 I made some calls to set up a visit for students from Gaston to do the same. Mr. Woodley arranged for a bus, and by April a group of KIPP students were off to Richmond. After touring the campus, the KIPP students spent the afternoon in Mike Davison's music class. Mike also invited them to attend a concert by the Latin jazz great Justo Almario; afterwards, they got to meet Almario backstage.

Later, I'd have more meetings with KIPP teachers and students, and would help to arrange scholarships and bus trips to competitions. Our foundation would confer our teacher award on Mr. Woodley and other dedicated educators at Gaston College Prep. But none of this would have happened if I hadn't decided to get out of New Hope. Having access to a car made my journey possible. Giving students access to a bus—so they can experience new and unfamiliar places—increased their opportunities, too.

I know that living in poverty isn't easy: I've watched students, parents and teachers maneuver the roadblocks in their path, and I can see it's hard work. But I also see them embrace change, no matter how uncomfortable it is, because they know that positive change will usually move them forward. At the very least, that embrace always leads to possibility.

For me, mourning was no easy game. It wasn't until I made that drive to North Carolina that I really began to move through my grief. That's when I realized that messing around in grief for too long, as necessary as it is, only reinforces the very emotions I was trying to escape. So find a reason to get out of the house. You don't have to go far. You could collect dresses in your hometown and deliver them to disadvantaged teen girls to make their prom really special.

Nor do you have to work alone. Because the Riedley's daughter had been a runner, her parents sponsored a Girls on the Run event. Partnering with a national organization helped them get started and gave Ginny and Roger an immediate entree to the non-profit world.

P.S. In 2013, Chevon Boone graduated from the University of Pennsylvania. We reconnected through her teaching job in New Jersey, and I asked her to speak to the first graduating class at one of our partner schools, Foundation Collegiate Academy, in Trenton. Chevon's extraordinary speech inspired the next potential leaders in the audience. So that first road trip I made to Gaston crossed many boundaries and, in the end, came full circle.

Here's an excerpt from "The Decision"—the poem Chevon wrote in fifth grade, inspired by Robert Frost. I heard her read it on that first visit to Gaston College Prep.

"In fifth grade two roads diverged and I was forced to decide
There was no turning back, but no reason to hide
Stay where it was simple or come to G.C.P.
You see, this was the choice that lay before me.

As I travel this road I'm setting all my dreams free
And it all started with one decision not to be ordinary.
Years from now it will be clear and everyone will know
In fifth grade, two roads diverged and the difference will
definitely show. "

Get out of the house.

Lead with your heart.

STEP SIX: ACT LOCALLY

Don't take on the burdens of the world. Begin the quiet outreach from your very vulnerable heart, in a familiar place. Your giving can be anonymous. Let's say you know an access ramp is needed for your church or community center. Build it. Even a simple, thoughtful gesture is meaningful. A nurse once told me that when bereaved parents sent a small gift to thank her for caring for their dying child, she felt appreciated and humbled.

If you lost your child to a terminal illness, you'll find inspiration at the ThereWithCare website. This non-profit provides services to families during a medical crisis: transportation, meals, home repair and sibling support. Some parents established programs within ThereWithCare to memorialize their children, and their stories will move you.

Respond to need close to home, especially so others who knew your loved one can participate, too. The Gutekunst family, friends in New Hope, helped us fill a large U-Haul truck with band instruments they donated. We delivered them to Trenton Central High School in New Jersey, where students from New Hope and Trenton unloaded the truck. On that snowy day in 2006, I felt we were doing something worthwhile.

Music with a Mission: World Water Day

I would have been content just to help support music programs across the river in New Jersey, but after we found Jonathan's poster about the PlayPump in Malawi, we decided to finish raising the money to build it. We couldn't travel to Africa, but we could address the issues around water rights that were important to our son, and we could do that right at home.

So once again, with the generous help of our friend Ian Kelly, we jumped in with music and multimedia. Luckily, Ian is just as much at home organizing a halftime show for the Super Bowl as a volunteer project at our high school. We produced a Water Heroes event with the school's environmental club for World Water Day in March 2009. Live entertainment was provided by the New Jersey high school musicians I'd met in Camden and at the Bonnie Brae School for at-risk boys in Liberty Corner. Even our New Hope mayor and the president of our county water company got involved. Listening to musical performances and watching trailers from two documentaries, *FLOW* and *Liquid Assets*, the audience learned about water rights and conservation. Everyone left with a reusable water bottle, and we raised most of the money needed to finish Jonny's fundraiser for PlayPumps International.

Water problems are very complex. In 2010, that well was built at the Mafe F. Primary School, in Malawi. Because the PlayPump is attached to a merry-go-round powered by students to deliver water from a well to a storage tank, it has the added benefit of keeping students in school. But a few years later, we learned that the PlayPump needed to spin all day long in order to provide enough water for a community. Because we weren't on site in Africa, we didn't

51

know that this delivery system had a high potential for failure. It wasn't easy for us to be accountable for our investment from a distance. While we'd responded locally by raising awareness about water issues (including the effects of fracking in a drilling state like Pennsylvania), we had no way to check up on the PlayPump installation in Africa.

But recently, we found another way to respond to the world water crisis in a part-time local way—in Mexico. We now live part of the year in the high desert in San Miguel de Allende, Mexico, where in 2017 we learned about a local group working on water issues. Caminos de Agua teams up with university collaborators to find realistic, low-tech solutions to procuring safe and healthy drinking water. We realized that this was another opportunity to continue our outreach. Here we can see the ceramic filters produced by Caminos de Agua, and we can visit the countryside easily to verify their work. It's clear that the aquifer is declining at an alarming rate, but we've met families who no longer consume arsenic because they now have access to rainwater collection systems. Using local water in their testing, Caminos de Agua developed four prototype systems and nine full-scale trials. I can do my part by writing a check.

Today, so many international NGOs (nongovernmental organizations) are doing crucial work: building medical clinics, providing shelter for refugees, offering micro-finance services to poor women. You need only partner with a successful one and then share their work with your community. To evaluate an NGO, consult Charity Navigator, which assesses the financial health of non-profits and discloses the percentage of income that goes toward programs. You'll have to decide for yourself if the charity is making an impact.

We are all this close to chaos, whether it's one step away from a permanently polluted aquifer or a school invaded by gunshots, two steps away from homelessness, three from losing control of our vote. But in these polarized times we tend to forget that we are capable and even closer to goodness, if we just believe we are.

The high school students who survived the school shooting in Parkland, Florida, responded to their loss with goodness and action. Only 38 days after the massacre at their school, those brave students became the positive activists behind the March for Our Lives, a massive nationwide rally for gun reform.

Step Seven: Vet Your Volunteers

At the beginning of your outreach, all you really need are supportive, non-judgmental friends with their sleeves rolled up, ready to work.

> *"I know there is strength in the differences between us. I know there is comfort, where we overlap."*
>
> — Ani DiFranco
> Singer-Songwriter

Two Perspectives

As our mission became public, the thoughtfulness of others grew. I learned that while some people are hard-wired for empathy, others are more sympathetic. Volunteers were helpful whatever their capacity to understand our loss, but until I recognized that emotional difference I sometimes had false expectations. It's important to understand the different traits when you step into philanthropy.

Sympathy, the older of the two terms, is the ability to express an understanding and to care about someone else's suffering. It's often associated with expressing condolences; it can feel like reading a Hallmark card. Sympathetic people may think that events, good or bad, happen for a reason. *They expect you to move on.*

Friends and strangers are concerned for you, but they may not have a shared perspective. Even if you repeat the details of your sorrow a hundred times, they still won't understand. Be prepared for this. The good thing is, they will listen.

Empathy, on the other hand, is felt. It's the ability to experience the feelings you are experiencing. Empathetic people are more likely to have lost a child, or perhaps a sibling when they were younger; they remember what they and their parents went through. They can see your situation from your perspective. *With time they only expect you to move forward.*

For me, empathy feels like listening to Oscar Peterson play "Love Ballade."

Don't confuse empathy with pity. You're more likely to have rapport with the empathetic person. That person isn't necessarily more sensitive than one who's hard-wired for sympathy, but tends to be more engaged, and as a result is more likely to commit to your cause.

Here are some other things I learned about working with volunteers. When you meet with people who are interested in helping, make your priorities and your expectations clear. Explain your mission and the purpose behind your work, and describe your program in detail. Before you decide if a potential volunteer is a good fit, ask if they have an appropriate talent or skill to share. Are they comfortable working solo, or would they rather partner with someone? How much time can they commit to your project?

If you make sure your volunteers can help meet the specific needs of your recipients, you're less likely to be disappointed.

Avoid dreamers, and sort out the talkers from the doers. Brainstorming can be helpful, but only after you get your feet wet.

Embrace yourself. If a dear friend doesn't understand that you still fall apart four years after the loss of your child, put your shield on.

STEP EIGHT: GET CLOSE

Step Eight is about transition. While you're maneuvering your way through your outreach and balancing the stages of grief, don't fail to stay close to the ones you love—your family, your friends. Take a break from your work to tend to your relationships.

I've read that many parents divorce after losing a child. Bob and I were lucky; our loss brought us closer together. And our older sons just accepted from the beginning that I would spend more time with a dead son than with them. Matthew and Brian were very patient as we defined their brother's memorial. But after several years we made fewer trips to the cemetery and became more present in *their* lives, trying to do normal family things.

Then get close to the community you want to support. Spend time there and get comfortable in it. Ask questions and leave your ego at the door. Decide if this is the place where you want to leave your handprint. Your reward comes from being there.

The Balancing Act

Try to connect your charitable deeds with the needs of the community. Meet people where they are and give them the help *they* need. Listen, don't judge.

Then start to prioritize your mission based on what you've experienced thus far. Decide who you want to get close to in your outreach and how to build on those relationships. When we first became involved with Foundation Academies in 2008, it was to lend financial support to their expanding orchestra program. But over the years, the more time I spent at this successful charter school in Trenton, the more we helped with their civic service learning class.

The social safety net seems to be fast eroding in modern America, but not in Kimby Heil's service learning class at Foundation Academies. Here high school juniors learn how to be responsible for their community and find ways to help. The class covers such issues as hunger, police relations, littering, crime, literacy and unemployment. In 2017, one group of students chose a simple project to help Trenton's homeless people: by offering them a home-cooked meal and a free haircut.

Intrigued, I visited the M Hair Salon to watch the class in action. While the students busily served meals and washed hair, I saw them overcoming the uncomfortable divide that had initially existed in the salon. The students listened, and learned about people's lives before they slept in a shelter. They engaged, with the hope of doing more and pulling as many souls into the lifeboat as possible.

As I watched this scene unfold, I was struck anew by the overwhelming needs in our society. But while I felt a deep compassion for the homeless people in the salon, I didn't feel a connection to them. Nor did I feel Jonny's presence.

That told me I wouldn't be an effective volunteer in this cause and made me realize the importance of setting limits for myself.

Your outreach needs to be a good fit for you. As you get closer to your cause you may become more vulnerable. If you feel uncomfortable with your efforts to help others, then perhaps your child isn't present. At the M Hair Salon in Trenton, I didn't hear music. I didn't feel that advocating for the homeless is work that Jonathan would have been involved in. Our work is rooted in mentoring young people. I was also reminded that we're a small family-run foundation, and I can't over-commit my time and our resources.

Still, I wanted to support this service program in some way, because it's a breeding ground for future social activists. Jonathan was a social activist. So we created a monetary award that would allow students to keep working in service as part of a paid summer job. We call it the TEAM award—for Trenton Entrepreneurs and Mentors. It makes me feel as if I'm sending angels out into the streets to do *their* work.

And that day in the hair salon reminded me to step in when our outreach *is* a fitting tribute to Jonathan. The message is simple: step in. Your work allows you to still be a parent to your child. This is how you heal. Simply hang on to your child in his "afterlife" and finish the work he would be doing if he were still alive.

Get close. Because, like me, you are still alive and able to do the work for your child. Like me, you will move into the best stage of grief: the gift of time.

And that's a blessing.

Grief never ends
but it changes.

It's a passage, not a place to stay.

Grief is not a sign of weakness,
nor a lack of faith.

It's the price of love.

—Author Unknown

Step Nine: Identify Your Mission

Mourning takes potential.
Knowing your limits should not be limiting.

There's no right or wrong way to grieve, and no right or wrong way to pay tribute.

For me, this step was the most nuanced. Take time to know your child and to personally define your mission, your response. When your good will journey begins, it will be so rewarding that it may seem intoxicating, even overwhelming. So take time at the start to understand what was important to your child and what gave his life meaning. Then memorialize him.

Crafting a mission statement for your outreach is very important. It will guide you and clarify your purpose, perhaps even years from now, at a time when you need to stay on message. But there's a reason why I didn't make writing the mission statement Step One. We learned what our mission should be through experience. I got my first glimpse of what philanthropy could really be for our family during that trip to Gaston, N.C.

This step into philanthropy really starts when you reluctantly write your child's obituary. From that point, the process of creating a tribute to our son evolved gradually. For me, it started by spending time in his room.

Tending His Shadow to Tend to Others

In those first few years, whenever I missed Jonny I made myself go to his bedroom—the room where I never heard music anymore. I'd take his wool socks and wrinkled clothes from the pile of dirty laundry and lay them out on the blue carpet to recreate a shadow of him. The hooded plaid jacket, a gift from his Aunt Carol last Christmas, would go on top; his rumpled brown corduroy pants on the bottom, with his work schedule for Farley's, the independent bookshop in town where all our sons worked, still stuffed in his right pocket.

I'd thumb through his philosophy books and Oberlin papers. I scribbled notes on the back of his wilderness first aid certificate. One by one, I stacked his music theory books and old Wes Montgomery scores in a neat pile next to the ghost of him.

This is how I wandered through his life, imagining he was still alive. At the time I thought I was mourning, but now I realize I was also looking for a way to memorialize our son in his foundation. In his shadow I sought a plan for recreating him on earth at age 19 and 23 and 35. What issues mattered most to him?

The book by his bedside was *The Man Who Planted Trees*, by Jean Giono. That made me think, "Maybe we should partner with a conservation group?" As I brushed the mud off the boots that had carried him through North Carolina's Pisgah Forest, I wondered, "Should we name a hut on the Appalachian Trail after him?" I thought of our three sons boogie-boarding together at the beach, shooting hoops and playing board games. "Should we support poor kids at summer camp?" I was waiting for a trigger to help clarify our mission. I longed to know, as I do for his brothers, what his future would have been.

Sitting in his room, I half-expected a response from my recreation of him. I remembered reading about the denial stage in one of the books on grief that our friends, Jock and Martha Gracey, had given us. I had to remind myself that Jonny wasn't *really* there—but maybe he felt my presence the way I could still feel him practicing in his room. If I listened, I could hear him, effortlessly playing Mozart's "Turkish March" on his guitar.

Though the sadness was beyond measure, it was a sadness I didn't want to lose, for fear of losing the memory of him.

I could still touch the remains of his life, clumsily resurrected in his room. His musty clothes smelled like the crocheted afghan throws on Grandma's couch. I thought about the last time he made English popovers with her and added too much salt. I'd forgotten how much he liked to cook. "Maybe we should feed people who are hungry?"

It was snowing out, so I placed his knit cap atop his jacket. As I got up to leave, an argument we'd had over politics raced through my mind. But then I thought I heard him calmly practicing Romberg's "Softly As In a Morning Sunrise." The melody seemed to echo through his lonely room and rest on his boot, tipped sideways with laces still in a knot.

Mourning takes work. But I wanted this grief to weigh on me and lead me to the right program in his name, the right scholarship—and it was better than not feeling him at all. The time I spent laying out the ghost of Jonny helped me focus. I remembered what he was all about. I took every last bit of him from those quiet encounters and tucked him into me.

Some 10 years later, that energy—the weight of Jonny's personality—remains at the core of our outreach. Without it I would just have become an estranged benefactor, doing good only by sitting at long conference tables and writing checks to strangers. While it took me more than 10 years to accept his death, it only took three years before I could wash his clothes and give them away. But thanks to those sobering visits to Jonny's room, I found a purpose.

I knew what I needed to do: Music with a mission. Getting out of that lonely room and taking his soul to the broken streets of Camden mended me.

With time you will embrace your mission, too. And when you do, believe that your work matters.

"...softly, as in a morning sunrise,
the light that gave you glory, will take it all away,
softly as it fades away, as it fades away..."
—Sigmund Romberg
Composer, 1887–1951

Mission and Money

The influences in Jonathan's life were clear,
    so identifying our mission was fairly straightforward.

    Nature was his teacher. Music was his voice.

However, writing the mission statement took more time
        than we expected and even more revisions.
    A few tightly edited lines have to hold a lot of purpose.

        Choose carefully.

The Jonathan D. Krist Foundation
promotes the study of music,
the humanities and the environment
by awarding scholarships and grants
to persons who have shown individuality
in their creative pursuits.

EIN 20-5317072

Step Ten: Hire Professionals

Even if you begin your outreach in an organic way, you still want it to grow with an over-arching vision. I learned very quickly that establishing a foundation by using a grassroots approach is like building a house without ever having done even a simple remodel on the den. You need to hire a lawyer to structure your charity and an accountant to file tax returns. These are the two jobs you don't want to mess up. Fortunately, we had expert help in both departments.

Managing Your Mission

A foundation or non-profit is a modern way of grieving—a very public response to your loss. We would have been woefully confused in the beginning without the kind guidance of our friend and lawyer, Peter Reiss, a partner at Clemons, Richter & Reiss PC in Doylestown, PA. He knew our son and understood what we wanted to accomplish: to formulate an appropriate tribute for Jonathan that would also help us deal with our unimaginable loss.

Here are some questions you might ask your lawyer.

1. What's the difference between a public foundation and a private one? What basic rules must be followed to avoid jeopardizing the tax-exempt status of either?

2. Can you offer some guidelines for choosing a board? What are the advantages and disadvantages of having board members outside the family?

3. What tips can you offer for writing a mission statement? If possible, you want to identify your mission in ten words or less. For example, the work of the Carter Center is stated simply as this: Wage peace, fight disease, build hope.

4. How do you know that a family is ready to commit time and resources to a memorial—and, the complications it might entail?

5. Do you ever recommend that, instead of establishing a charity of their own, parents join forces with an existing community foundation or open a donor-advised fund?

6. How can parents build flexibility into their planning? Most people know little about legal entities; besides which, their state of mourning can obscure their decision-making abilities. They may want to change the direction of their mission.

7. If parents decide at the start to limit their public tribute to a fixed period of time, what is required to close a charitable entity when the time is up?

8. How can we insure that our work outlives us?

One advantage of starting a non-profit organization is that it can continue long after the founders are gone. I saw that for myself on a visit to the Hospital of St. Cross, in Winchester, which started in 1136 and is one of the oldest charities in England. It still cares for the elderly, and is so steeped in tradition that it has never stopped offering bread and ale to any passing travelers who request it.

If you're daunted by the idea of forming and managing your foundation yourself, outsourcing is an option. Scholarship America, a nonprofit group based in Minnesota, designs and manages memorial funds for a fee based on the complexity and customization. CharitySmith National Society of Memorial Funds is another possibility.

Follow these basic steps to form your non-profit 501(c)(3) corporation.

1. Choose a name for your charitable organization.

2. File articles of incorporation as a private or public entity and post them publicly in your local newspaper.

3. Apply for IRS and state tax exemption. (Warning: The application runs about 110 pages.) Once you're approved, you'll receive a determination letter with your assigned exempt identification number (EIN).

4. Draft bylaws.

5. Appoint directors.

6. Hold your first annual meeting and record minutes.

7. With your EIN, open a checking account to pay initial expenses and deposit donations.

8. File Form 990 with the IRS annually (usually by June of the following year).

"Giving from the heart and the head changes the equation."
– Peter Singer, Founder
The Life You Can Save

Managing Money in Your Charity

For most investors, emotions tend to override rational thinking about money. That's true even before the loss of a child—and money matters take on an even more complex dynamic with grief. You must act responsibly, but you shouldn't feel pressured to be an expert.

In the beginning, just think of money as a tool to meet your goals. It will grow by itself in a tax-exempt setting. You'll want to open a brokerage account so you can invest some of the initial donations. Your job isn't to become a financial wizard; it's to protect the good intentions of your donors. They don't want to know how much money you've accrued, they want to know what you're doing with it.

Decide how much you need to cover expenses and fund your first few good deeds. Put the rest of the money in a dividend-paying ETF or a proven low-cost, balanced fund like Vanguard Wellington. Start a website for the foundation, and then set up an account with Network for Good so any online donations can be deposited directly to your brokerage account.

Write a personal note to every donor with a thank-you receipt that includes your EIN (employer identification number). The message might include language like "Thank you for your recent donation. This letter acknowledges that the amount of goods or services provided were zero. Therefore your total contribution is considered a tax-deductible gift."

Keep concise but consistent records, including board-meeting minutes. Send a personalized annual letter to inform friends and donors of your good deeds. Share specific examples and don't be bashful; non-profit organizations are agents of change in many communities.

When you meet with your lawyer you want to learn about giving well—that is, making the most of your time, your commitment, and the donations you receive. In the summer of 2006, I was in a muddled state when I first sat across from Peter. I just wanted to create an entity with our son's name on it. I thought a foundation was more fluid than a grave marker and one way to keep a grasp on Jonathan's life.

But I didn't know how a foundation would work or what it really meant going forward. It wasn't until about ten years later, after I'd read books by Peter Drucker and Peter Singer, that I began to realize how our little charity could become my life's work. If this transformation happens to you, start thinking about that legacy thing, no matter how modest.

Common Challenges

"Never doubt that a small group
of thoughtful, committed citizens
can change the world.
Indeed, it is the only thing that ever has."

—Margaret Mead
Anthropologist, 1901–1978

Introduction: Ten Common Challenges

Some of the challenges you'll encounter in your outreach will probably be the same as those we experienced. In this section I'll share our stories from the field, in hopes that my insights will help you overcome similar roadblocks.

We had to learn to keep our grief and our good will in balance. This is no easy task, since grief continually creeps in unexpectedly. To maintain my balance, I had to accept these two rules:

Rule #1 - Give. Nothing I do will ever bring our child back. I can only give his future to others. Effective outreach, for any grieving parent, is about taking strength from the simple deed of giving.

Rule #2 - Take. Everything I do in this charitable regard leaves me emotionally vulnerable. If I'd chosen to insulate myself and shut out the pain, I would never have experienced the unexpected joy I found. Effective healing, for any grieving parent, is about taking comfort from the people we meet along the way.

STARTING A PROGRAM FROM SCRATCH

The Jazz Academy at Solebury School

In the cluttered music room at Creative Arts High School in Camden, N.J., I watch the students busily pack up books and trombones, anticipating the closing bell. It's not that they're eager to get outdoors on this warm spring afternoon in 2010; instead, they're excited that professors from the prestigious Oberlin Conservatory have come from Ohio to visit their school.

Back then, Creative Arts was in a rundown four-story brick building on South Sixth Street. The chain-linked fence surrounding the school marks the perimeter for hope in this abandoned, drug infested neighborhood. But for these eager teenagers, this building is a safe, creative haven; a place to overcome the threats of poverty. This is where they have chosen to create a better life for themselves. And they do. Their jazz band consistently wins regional and international competitions and outsiders have begun to take notice.

Once the Oberlin professors have arrived, I watch with pride as they interview the school's band director, Jamal

78

Dickerson, a man who's very committed to improving the choices for Camden's young people.

Suddenly the unmistakable sound of a gunshot shatters the air. The room falls silent. The shot came from the alley behind the school. The students quickly file out of the classroom to line up in the hallway, but I stand there looking like a deer in the headlights; I've only ever seen this kind of stuff on television. The principal's calm voice comes over the PA system: the school is in lockdown, an all-too-familiar drill in Camden. I move away from the windows.

One shot was all it took. A woman in the alley is bleeding out, a victim of being in the wrong place at the wrong time. We don't know her name. She simply got in the way of an angry man with a handgun who'd robbed the convenience store where the school kids stop for snacks. Now the school is strangely quiet. The students are lined up in the hall waiting, almost as if this were normal. On South Sixth Street, it is.

I'll never forget that day. It was a vivid reminder of why I was present.

I'd met Jamal Dickerson two years earlier, when I delivered band instruments to the school. (That was in thanks to James McBride for participating in our video about water rights. And James himself ended up at the school because he volunteered to give lessons to a very talented music student, Alex Cummings.)

On that first visit Jamal had asked for my help. He and Hassan Sabree, his best friend and fellow music teacher in Camden, wanted to start a summer program to fill the one week in August when his students were idle, and most likely to be tempted by wrong decisions in Camden. Or, as Jamal bluntly asked, "Help me save kids from prisons, caskets and the corner." Together we created a leadership/mentoring program, disguised as an overnight music camp, that lasted for five very creative years.

It was during this time I successfully channeled my despair into action. This is when I finally rose from my mourning. It would be the best and most stressful five years of our outreach. But it would also be the most productive stage of my healing.

*In 2012, jazz great Barry Harris came from New York City
to teach master classes at Jazz Academy.
(He's the octogenarian in the grey shirt.)*

This is what I learned about starting a program from scratch:

Buy in completely. Because when you do, everyone else will.

Don't let a lack of experience stand in your way. I'm not a musician or an educator, but our son Matthew is both. He would guide us, as Bob and I were definitely punching above our weight. But that didn't really matter, because we bought in completely. To start the camp I *only* had to find a safe place, with fresh air and warm meals, for 40 or 50 kids for a week. Luckily, after several calls and letters to prep schools and campsites in our area, I found that place through the generous support of the Solebury School in New Hope, PA.

The program began as a weekend retreat in late June 2010; by July 2011 it had expanded into a weeklong curriculum. Living in dorms and studying on a bucolic campus encouraged students to consider college in their future. We named the camp Jazz Academy at Solebury School.

Not knowing the rules or the expectations can work in your favor. At least it did for me, because I never lost sight of the fact that for these students, any experience that summer would be better than their choices in Camden.

A major key to success lies in finding volunteers who share your goals. We were fortunate to connect with Brian and Marci Alegant, faculty members at Oberlin Conservatory who brought their expertise and their students to help shape our program. They did the teaching, and encouraged everyone to take musical risks, especially the horn players. They started each day at camp with a morning choral class followed by a meditation exercise. In no time, everyone on campus was attending Marci's morning singing class, including me.

Thanks to people like the Alegants, this wasn't your ordinary jazz program.

Another suggestion: make two budgets.

One budget is for the costs you can't avoid—in our case, food and a cook. The second budget is for the variable line items. Be prepared with a big check to cover the fixed costs, and then decide whether you're willing to beg and borrow for the rest. If you don't want to take the gamble, see if you can partner with an existing program whose costs are known.

Jamal Dickerson brought the most value to the program; the curriculum, his students and his volunteer teachers.

His school district paid for the bus that brought the kids from Camden to New Hope. To help cover other expenses, I recruited some students from our area who could pay full tuition; Camden students who lived outside public housing were asked to pay what they could. The balance was covered by the ticket sales from a concert that all the students performed at Havana, a landmark music club in New Hope.

To help figure out what you want to accomplish, draw up a list of five or six reasonable goals—and hope that at least half of them can be met. This was our list:

1. Find students from different socioeconomic and music backgrounds.

2. Show students that they have choices, and demonstrate what those choices look like through role modeling with college students.

3. Let students enjoy the rewards of healthy food, fresh air and a safe place to run track.

4. Increase the students' chord-phrasing, sight-reading and book-reading skills.

5. Extend Jazz Academy to "teachers only" in the form of a sabbatical.

As we laid our plans, we learned to follow the cardinal rule for jam sessions: don't be a solo hog. In other words, don't rely on your own hype.

And finally, know your own personality. If you're not easygoing, if you stiffen up in the face of adversity and change, don't try to wing it. Instead, partner with an existing program that feels familiar to you.

However you choose to participate in the greater good, ask yourself—as I did on that day of the South Sixth Street shooting—what if I stood by and did nothing? When you know the answer, and the answer starts to fill the hole in your heart, you'll know you're ready to start a program from scratch. And if you go for it, have the courage to buy in completely.

THE FIVE-YEAR REUNION

During one summer session at Jazz Academy, the students watched *Thunder Soul*, a 2010 documentary produced by Jamie Foxx. It tells the story of the Kashmere Stage Band, which rose to fame in the 1970s in Houston. Thirty-five years after the musicians left school, they returned to honor their retired band teacher with one more concert. Foxx had a similar music experience growing up in Terrell, Texas, and this film reinforces the value of the arts in education. By the end of the screening there wasn't a dry eye in the room; many of the students knew they had the same kind of mentor in someone like Jamal Dickerson.

I can't wait 35 years for a reunion. I'll be dead by the time Jamal and Hassan retire, like Conrad "Prof" Johnson did in the movie. But 2020 will mark five years since our program ended, and a five-year reunion seems like the right thing to do.

I was convinced of that when Josh Lee, a former student at Jazz Academy, came up to reintroduce himself to me at a high school jazz festival in Camden in 2018. Obviously more mature, he's now the assistant band director for Pennsbury High School in Fairless Hills, PA. I'd forgotten his name, but I did remember he played baritone sax. That's when I realized I wanted to know what had become of the rest of the talented and compassionate young people who passed through Jazz Academy.

I must continue to piece together the puzzle and see what happens next.

EXPANDING YOUR MISSION

Our "Stand Partners" Program

You accomplish two things by partnering with an existing program. You can assume your role as an advocate immediately, and you'll have an expert on hand to guide you. That's what happened to us when we decided to support the music program at Foundation Academies, the Trenton charter school for grades K–12.

Foundation Academies opened in 2007 with only a middle school; back then its orchestral program had 80 students. Before the founding music director gave out any instruments, he'd hand every student a Styrofoam cup. Those who succeeded in carrying that cup for seven days without damaging or losing it would prove they could be responsible for an expensive violin or cello. Matthew and I heard this story when we visited the school in late 2008, and we bought in completely.

Unlike at Jazz Academy, we didn't have to find the space, the students or the instructors. All we had to do was help the teachers strengthen their existing program. In the beginning we simply filled requests, providing money to build a portable storage closet for the double basses, cover expenses for off-site concerts at a local college auditorium, send students to music camp and buy violins for the expanding student body.

FINDING A FIT

Eventually, partnering with an established program allowed us to expand our mission beyond just covering expenses. I wanted to help their staff establish a program to encourage the serious musicians at Foundation Academies. The school now has more than 1,000 students, and they're all required to take music class. Like any required class, not everyone wants to be there. To encourage the students who do love music and are eager to attend, we developed an honors-like program called Stand Partners.

(The name comes from orchestra musicians who sit side by side during a performance, sharing a music stand. The idea behind this program is that two students work as a team.)

Stand Partners began as a master class and fundraising concert with Concordia Chamber Players, an acclaimed chamber music group based in New Hope. Concordia's founder is Trenton native Michelle Djokic, a talented cellist who has made a point of sharing her knowledge with the students at Foundation Academies whenever she's in town. And for the first two years of the program, we arranged for the students to perform with Djokic's colleagues at Ellarslie Mansion, the Italianate villa that houses the Trenton City Museum.

Michelle Djokic teaching Nelly Sanchez in her master class.

Since then Stand Partners has added a collaboration with the music department at West Chester University, a state school in West Chester, PA. We pay the tuition for motivated students to attend their one week classical program each July. For these young musicians this is not a reward, this is fulfillment. Like the students at Jazz Academy, the Trenton students get an opportunity to live on a college campus and benefit from an intense week of instruction.

I didn't have to plan the Stand Partners program from scratch so I wasn't distracted by logistics. I have time to observe and to get to know the orchestra students. I look for their college scholarship applications in their senior year. I listen to students express themselves as a duet, both exactly in tune and in rhythm, but learning new fingering and phrasing from each other. I watch them negotiate the little things, like where to place the music stand and their chairs.

Turning the pages, and doing it on time, takes patience. I notice which students mess up, and which ones are writing reminders about sharps and flats (and pizza delivery numbers) in the margins of their sheet music. Most importantly I watch them develop unconditional support for each other. When they're performing together on stage, Stand Partners hear the best and the worst of each other—and that's a secret only the two of them share.

I could have easily accomplished good deeds just by writing checks. But then I would have missed the personal serendipity that followed Jonny's death.

ANGEL'S WINGS

A month before I came to Foundation Academies, I'd had a similarly gratifying experience. I connected with Little Kids Rock—a nationwide nonprofit that trains public school music teachers and provides all the resources needed to run pop/rock-based music education classes. In November 2008, I visited PS 11 in the Highbridge neighborhood of the Bronx with David Wish, founder of Little Kids Rock. David told me about his group's community outreach and how they vet recipients, and his insights helped clarify my commitment to Foundation Academies.

It helped that I knew the Foundation Academies directors would always include music in their curriculum. Elsewhere, music is often the first discipline to be cut from a budget—but it's the one that keeps many kids in school. I learned that at PS11, the absentee rate dropped by 40 percent after the Little Kids Rock program started. At the end of my day there, I watched as these elementary school kids all walked out the doors with small black guitar cases strapped on their backs. The school superintendent called the guitars "angel's wings," carrying the kids through urban blight and safely home. If I had just mailed off a check to David Wish, I would never have experienced that inspiring moment.

Angel's wings. When I heard that simple observation, I realized we could also give wings to the serious music students at Foundation Academies. Help support one school, with one tool—music—and see where it goes. In effect, we became a "stand partner."

FALSE EXPECTATIONS

Live What Still Lives in You

As you begin your outreach, keep your expectations simple. Focus on your mission—it comes first. While some nonprofits quickly become very productive, don't expect yours to take off immediately. I always expect my best ideas, which are really Jonny's ideas, to turn into something much bigger. But I've learned that the reward comes in small gifts, like witnessing the personal growth of the people you help. Here are a few other things I've learned.

Expect to be tired. Especially in the beginning, because you are embracing your work from weakness.

Be realistic. I still tend to overthink my capabilities. You will too, because your loss is so big. I know that hiring student musicians to produce World Water Day assemblies in schools around the country is a good idea, but it's not a realistic one. I know that building a grant program to reinforce the service projects of our Jonny Scholars is a natural progression in our mission, but I'd need a paid or even a volunteer staff to get it done.

Be surprised. I expected more from some of the people who actually knew our son. I didn't expect as much as I got from strangers. Nor did I expect the amount of money we would receive in donations to our cause. Don't be surprised if nobody remembers your name or vocation. They will remember your good deeds in your child's name; and the way you adapted to tragedy.

Be accountable. Expect to never forget the people who care enough to encourage you. And also expect to be held accountable for other people's money and good will. I've always been good at handling money, so I wasn't intimidated by the prospect of managing the business of philanthropy— I had no false expectations there.

Be cautious. If you're organizing a public event like a bike race, make sure it's properly insured. Don't expect participants to be sympathetic because of your loss, and forgive you if something goes wrong. You don't need a liability in your fundraiser.

Be anonymous. I do need to see our son's name in public. I expect his foundation logo to follow me from the band room to a mountain trail. But if you don't expect or need public recognition, give quietly, on your own terms and unencumbered. The simple act of giving is the real tribute.

Remain hopeful. I don't know what to expect for the future. I just know that there *is* one for me because of our decision to memorialize our son.

Many people said Jonny was like a bridge, connecting people of different backgrounds and ages through music.

91

At the start of our outreach I became the promoter, the fundraiser and the program director, trying to build that bridge from New Hope to deprived urban neighborhoods on the other side of the Delaware River. With time I realized that I am the bridge, and this is what I was supposed to be doing all along.

In late 2009 I heard Clarence Clemmons, the legendary sax player with the E Street Band, say something that stuck with me: "Live what lives in you." Clarence was playing at a Little Kids Rock fundraiser at B.B. King's club in New York City, and those words are still helping me stay the course without false expectations.

"If you deny who you are
you will never be able to go into life
and fulfill your purpose. "

— Desi Shelton-Seck
Founder, Camden Repertory Theatre

FAILURE TO LAUGH

For years I lost my smile, but it finally came back to me during a trip to Ohio in 2009. I was with colleagues in a crowded, muggy van, and I laughed out loud for so long I was propelled one giant step forward out of grief. One day I hope you'll have a big lift from mourning like mine.

Hassan Sabree (in black shirt) is just as surprised as everyone else as we head to the airport.

My Lucky Ride

He was a stranger, but I'd seen him earlier in the day as I walked along Morgan Street in Oberlin, Ohio. He was trimming holly hedges, with his big beige van parked in a driveway. I was staying nearby at the Hotel at Oberlin, and now I was waiting with colleagues for a limo to take us to the airport.

It was 2011, and I was here with teachers, a band director and a high school principal—to help the dean at the Oberlin Conservatory of Music develop his Music in America initiative. In every way, this trip was about Jonathan. His death had set this ball rolling, bringing inner-city students and their teachers to bucolic Oberlin.

When it got to be 45 minutes past our pickup time, it was clear that the limo service had abandoned us. I ran back down Morgan Street to reel Hank, or whatever his name was, into our emergency.

He wore a once-white T-shirt covered in sweat and food stains, and reeked of freshly cut grass and cigarette smoke. But van keys jangled in the pocket of his faded plaid shorts, and I knew those keys—and Hank—were our only chance to make our flights.

Before he could object, I'd jumped into the van's front seat. My first order of business was to convince him that there were 10 passengers waiting at the hotel, and they'd be willing to part with a good bit of cash to get to Cleveland's Hopkins International on time.

I rolled down the windows to break the cloud of heavy, moist air, made all the more cloying by the grape jam that dripped from a half-eaten sandwich on the driver's seat. I scooped his lunch into a napkin and nodded to signal him to hurry up. Both Hank and his old Ford may have been a

94

little out of date and in need of a steam cleaning, but Hank was quickly on board.

As soon as we rounded the corner, Ron, Jamal, Hassan, Patricio, Erika and Emily, as well as a stray "Obie" student, all gratefully jumped into the van. Maybe they thought I actually knew Hank, but for some reason, these otherwise sensible people trusted me—and Hank. When they realized I didn't know him at all, the fun began.

We were late, so Hank drove at a breakneck speed. Despite his loose interpretation of traffic laws, we managed to avoid both mayhem and the Ohio state troopers. All the while we were tweeting photos back to the dean and his staff, who'd assumed we were already on our way back to the coast. Maybe it was panic, or maybe it was the joy of giving up control, but as Hank careened towards Cleveland we laughed louder and longer than any of us had in a long, long time.

All the while I thought of our sweet Jonathan, the catalyst for this whole impulsive escapade. The ride had such an air of mischief and rebellion that I felt as if Jonathan was right there beside me, laughing along. I could hear him whisper, "You're going to be okay, Mom."

After Jonny's car accident, I would never have allowed myself to be so distracted in a moving vehicle, or given up control to a total stranger. Jonathan had died in the dark in a fast-moving vehicle, and every night since then I'd taken that painful ride over and over, digging through the emotional wreckage that was left behind. I never drove at night for fear of slipping into melancholy and oncoming traffic. It only takes one distraction to blur the dividing yellow line: rain on the windshield, a moody Coltrane solo on the radio, or the image of Jonny in the passenger seat, tapping out a 6/8 beat on the glove-compartment door. No, I knew enough to explore my sorrow at home, safely behind closed doors.

But five years later, a playful van ride with a guy named Hank gave me back the gift of laughter. It was one giant step out of grief, and just what I needed.

Accepting Your Fate

Many parents have lost children. Over 57,000 children under age 19 die every year in the United States. Each year over 3500 babies die from sudden infant death syndrome. In America, at least 1,300 children die from gun wounds annually. Over one million civilian and military parents on both sides lost their sons and daughters in the undeclared war in Vietnam.

Worldwide 100,000 young people a year die from cancer; 1,000 people under age 25 die from road accidents every day. Our son was one of those statistics. This was his fate. Honoring his life has become mine.

The weight of losing a child stays with every parent forever. That weight can be a blessing as well as a curse. It was a blessing for me because, in those first few years after his death, it gave me the sense of Jonathan's presence. I was pushed away from the sad stuff of life and leaned into hope when I knew I could finish what was important to our son.

Even when the physical and emotional burden seemed too heavy to bear, still I tried to embrace it. I realized this crushing weight was the form that the memory of his life would take. In time, I learned to accept my fate and carry the weight of Jonny's death in a good way.

Dead Weight

You too will learn how to carry the weight of your child's life into your outreach and believe you are making a difference. It's not just magical thinking: it has energy and purpose. It feels present.

In the first year after Jonathan's death I felt tired and vulnerable, but I was never irrational. I'm certain I *felt* Jonny. His hands followed mine on the piano keys when I played Billy Joel's "So It Goes." (When he was alive we'd connected through this melody, based on an old hymn.) And one time I caught a glimpse of him behind our house, on the stepping-stones he'd placed in Ingham Creek. It was that moment that inspired me to support the camping trip for at-risk boys at the Bonnie Brae School in Liberty Corner, NJ.

Embracing his presence allows me to feel him still, wherever the sorrow takes me—usually to a wonderfully noisy band room. But inevitably it leads to another year without him, marked off by placing a Christmas wreath on his grave.

This weight from a child's death feels different from other losses I've known. I didn't feel the same crushing burden when my parents died, or my oldest brother. Maybe it's because they were older, and they'd had full lives; their deaths felt like they followed a normal sequence. Closing the casket on them was like turning the last page of a satisfying book. I only lost a part of my past when they died, the part where we had interacted.

But when our son died, I lost his future, and our future. The book that would have been his life was snatched from my hands before it was finished. Now I need to finish writing it.

While the direction of our outreach was clear from the start, it is his life, his uncanny awareness at an early age of life's indifference and inequalities, that helps me stay the course. The trick is to focus my anger and figure out how to balance death, resentment and good will.

It took time for me to be able to bear the weight of our son. It pushed me forward. Eventually, like so many bereaved parents before me, I learned to accept his fate, and now my fate.

The same weight has pushed many other parents into action, such as those who have lost children to gun violence. They are the voices of Everytown for Gun Safety, founded in 2014 to advocate for commonsense reforms to help prevent future tragedies. Perhaps they'll be as successful in preventing deaths as the parents involved in Mothers Against Drunk Driving (MADD). Candy Lightner, who founded MADD, felt compelled to take action after losing her daughter Cari in 1980. The deadly toll of 25,000 people killed by drunk drivers that year has since been cut in half.

The same weight pushed Alison Malmon into action after her older brother, a Columbia University student suffering from depression, ended his life. In 2001 she formed Active Minds to change the conversation about mental health on college campuses. Some people still treat mental illness like a moral failing instead of a brain disease. Her outreach in Brian's name is erasing that stigma and serves as a model for society.

Twelve years have passed, and the sound and scent of Jonathan are gone. But his soul is still present, and his name remains in our plans. I am humbled by the responsibility.

He walks around with me. This is my fate. I let his humor, his complex spirit, and his frustrating politics guide me. His music taught me how to listen, but his life taught all of us how to step up from the zero point.

So I carry him with me, because the weight of him helped me create the foundation.

> *What lies behind us*
> *and what lies before us*
> *are tiny matters*
> *compared to what lies within us.*

—Oliver Wendell Holmes, Sr.
Physician, poet, professor, 1809–1894

Planning an Exit Strategy

It's hard to consider ending a nonprofit established to honor a life that ended too soon. But if you don't have successors who are willing to take it over, you must consider what's best when you're no longer present to do the work. The exit strategy is a plan for your immediate family, your donors and the people you help in your child's name. It's not a second death; it's a plan.

I hadn't thought about a long-term plan until Ginny Riedley mentioned hers on the night of the award ceremony. Her remarks gave me pause. As I stepped onstage that evening, a decade of mourning suddenly raced through my mind. It's a good thing I'd made notes for my presentation; once again, a trusty index card kept me from meandering into grief in front of strangers.

Shelf Life

Our family tradition continues. It's 2016 and I'm sitting in the lobby outside the New Hope Solebury High auditorium, waiting to go back on the same stage where Jonathan once led debates and all our sons received their high school diplomas. At tonight's senior awards ceremony, another capable student will add his name to our "signature gui-tar"—the Paul Reed Smith cherry-red guitar we'd kept in Jonny's name, that each of our scholarship students signs in turn.

Ten years ago I wished I'd screamed at the sight of our son's dead body on the hospital gurney, screamed like Brian did when he fell on his brother's grave and pounded out his piercing cries. Ten years later, I'm still waiting to scream and say it isn't so. But it is.

As I wait, I think about how walking on stage at this school still feels like walking the plank with some kind of noose around my neck. But it isn't; we're here helping students who need help. The value of our monetary award is hard to measure—it's an investment in these students' future, and that's it. I tell myself that this might be what Jonathan would be doing if he were alive—mentoring stu-dents through music.

I'm reminded that out of death came life; service to others, unconditionally. So staying in this philanthropy role is good for me. I have some control: I choose the work I do for him, in places that I like, too—a protected forest, an orchestra rehearsal hall. I think it puts me in Jonny's radar, so he can find me.

I look around and think it's good to be in familiar places so I can still feel our son. At least that's what I tell myself. You will too. If Jonathan's spirit returned, he'd know where to find us. We still live where he lived and breathe the same air he breathed.

Every year in May, a number of other bereaved parents also take their turn on this stage in New Hope, trying to keep the hopeful memory of their child alive. I'm sitting with Ginny Riedley, whose daughter Tara died two years after Jonathan. From the day Ginny sat in our living room seeking my advice in 2008, she and Roger have done so much to help others. But now, she tells me, they've decided not to stay in the game—10 years after Tara's death, they're ending their work in her name.

"Everything has a shelf life," Ginny explains. "And Tara would want me to get my life back. When I retire from my job it'll be time to end the fundraisers, the events and awards." I nod, but I'm bewildered by the prospect of an end, closure; the idea of not being held accountable.

But Ginny *is* still accountable. She honors her daughter's life every day. For her, for me, for all the bereaved parents here, there's no time stamp on our kindness. We have this "child who predeceased us" badge in common, and we line up as loyal mothers longing for only one thing: to keep our balance by helping others. So will you.

How else will we keep our children present?

Now it's my turn to step up to the podium where, in 2006, the principal announced Jonathan's death to a startled and unbelieving crowd. But tonight is different. Tonight I'm thinking about the millions of bereaved parents around the world who have stepped up before me.

First, I speak of the good deeds done by the former students who have died. I say each of their names in turn, so their mothers can hear them. One by one, over the years, all those names were spray-painted on the memorial boulder in front of the school: the Jamies, Thomases, Taras, Jonathans and Ethans of our town. That is the school tradition. The boulder is still there. Their mothers are reminded every day that their child lost that chance to be a kid, to rebel, to fall in love, to have their vote counted, to grow old. These mothers need to hear their child's name included in the conversation.

I see Jamie's mother give me a nod and wipe her eyes. Jamie had just finished maritime training and was about to start a job teaching sailing at the Bitter End Yacht Club on Virgin Gorda. He was on St. John waiting for his final working papers when he was murdered. Her husband brought their son home from an island paradise where the crime was covered up.

As I announce our latest Jonny Scholar, Jake Dupont, I think of how he and all the other students I interviewed hold the promise of fixing our incredible but complex world. I'm grateful for them all, and I'm aware that I would never have known them if it weren't for Jonathan's death.

When I speak about Jake, I don't list the requirements for getting a check from our foundation; nor do I brag about his GPA or his track trophies. I say what I really want to say: I talk about meeting Jake when he was in seventh grade, attending our Jazz Academy with the brother of his best friend, Ethan Toohey, who died that summer. Jake gets it from the heart and the head, so I mention how he helps the underdog, sleeves rolled up, unnoticed, doing volunteer work and getting the job done. I talk about how he quietly helped Ethan's brother get through Ethan's death from cancer. For Jake, like me, the only way out of his own grief was through it.

Jade Greene, our first Jonny Scholar, joins us on stage. She holds up our signature guitar, with 37 other names already inscribed on its shiny red body. Jake adds his name. When he's done, I tell him how much I appreciated our talks about bravery. I was humbled when Jake told me how it felt to watch his best friend slowly lose his fight with cancer.

I tell Jake that the scholarship isn't a gift, *he* is the gift. People in the audience sigh. I kiss him the way Europeans kiss each other and thank him, there on the stage decorated with bouquets of yellow flowers. Then I leave.

As I walk up the aisle I recognize familiar faces—teachers, an old neighbor, our retired banker. I slowly turn left out the auditorium door, closing it quietly behind me. Alone in the parking lot, I stand still for a few minutes, head tilted down. I cross my arms over my heart and—finally—I scream.

LETTING GO

Our older sons call me a force of nature, and that helps me stay engaged. But really, I've shared so little of this what-we're-doing-as-a-family-in-Jonny's-name stuff *with* my family. It's unrealistic to think I can; they're at work on their own lives.

Still, I wish our sons could meet all the students, teachers, parents and grandmothers who climbed into my heart. I feel more useful at the schools in Camden and Trenton than I do in my privileged zip code across the river. I'm helping eager students whose best shot for a decent, rigorous education is to win a lottery. My work in these places feels more like the work Jonathan would be doing, if he could. And being in these places reminds me that I've never been hungry.

Following the story at my feet is all I know to do. And now I'm facing the question: Is our mission sustainable without me? Maybe Ginny was right when she talked about shelf life—maybe the work will eventually go stale.

That day of the awards ceremony was exactly when I realized that our family needs an exit strategy. It was the one lesson in philanthropy I'd failed to recognize; the end. In the beginning I dreamed that our outreach would become a family heirloom, like a stitched quilt or photo album we'd pass on to Jonny's brothers when we're old and feeble. But realistically, the only heirloom we'll leave is that shiny red Paul Reed Smith guitar covered with signatures. So we must stay connected to the people who have signed the guitar.

One day Bob and I will have that insightful "legacy" talk with our sons, and then we'll let go, just as Ginny did. We'll leave more of the work to them. By that time maybe they will have children of their own, and they'll understand how their grandfather's simple act of kindness took on a life of its own. I've finally accepted that making a plan for the possible end to our work is only one more challenge, a strategy, and not another death.

ONE YEAR LATER

I met with Ginny Riedley at the New Hope and Solebury library to share the first draft of this book with her. Recently, the Riedleys donated money to help remodel a worn children's room in the basement of the library. Sitting on tiny chairs in this charming, magical refuge, Ginny and I talked about our children and the work we do in their names.

Although Ginny and Roger had decided to eventually end their fundraising and events for Tara's foundation, they found something they'd been looking for since the beginning: a lasting visible tribute to their daughter's presence in our community. In this lovely children's room, Tara's name is proudly marked on a memorial plaque beside the bookshelves where all can see it, and where it will always be read and spoken out loud.

This room is where Tara, like many other young people, was inspired to read and look around her; this room helped mold the person she was to become. This is where her parents unexpectedly found closure to their mourning. Perhaps they would have reached this "aha" moment without their nine years of outreach. Or perhaps this beautiful memorial means more to them because they had already done so much to keep Tara present.

This passage from the inspirational lessons in the book *Oh, the Places You'll Go!* is inscribed on Tara's plaque. Let it guide you when it comes to all this planning stuff.

"You have brains in your head.
You have feet in your shoes.
You can steer yourself any direction you choose!"

—Theodor Geisel (Dr. Seuss)
1904–1991

Leaving Your Handprint

At a certain age you start to wonder how you will be re-membered. I'm at that age. I'd like to leave reminders of our Foundation work in places that outlive me, a place where causes that are important to our family will continue to be supported.

Where do we leave our family handprints?

As a mother, I need to find the Foundation's "home" -- and some continuity for Jonathan's brothers — before I am gone. Every bereaved parent knows there are no guaran-tees in life. Even though we've accepted loss, the magical thinking, the dreaming and longing never leaves us. So I kept looking for a place as old as the trees and as secure as my children's love for me.

When he was a junior in high school Jonathan attended the Outdoor Academy, a semester-long program in North Carolina. Those rigorous months in the natural world shaped him just as much as the years he spent in music rehearsals. So during the last few years I researched and visited a number of outdoor education programs and envi-ronmental centers to find one that would be a good fit for our mission.

I was looking for a place where we can spend time as a family now, and where our sons can continue our foundation outreach in the future. It would be a rustic spot that could provide some tranquility in their busy lives, and allow them to volunteer while they're on site. But while all the organizations I considered are doing admirable work, none of them felt like a lasting fit. Then, during a random conversation with a man at a recycling center in Maine, I learned about the Lacawac Sanctuary in northern Pennsylvania.

When I paid a visit to check it out, I found the same hopeful spirit that Jean Giono wrote about in *The Man Who Planted Trees*, a fable about one man's work to restore the earth. I walked down a path on the carefully preserved 550-acre biological field station that led to a small, pristine glacial lake. There a profiling buoy was collecting data. I imagined our sons, older and confident, walking the same trails and supporting the work of future scientists, artist residencies and conservation.

I knew my search was over. At Lacawac Sanctuary, the natural environment is the inspiration for conservation and creative pursuits. It's located in the shadow of the Appalachian Trail, where Jonathan had planned to start hiking with his brother on the day he died. Had fate worked out differently in May 2006, Matthew and Jonathan would have passed right by these mature woods on their way north.

And my arrival was timely, as their trustees plan to convert the original founder's home into an environmental center for STEM education (science, technology, engineering and math). Besides being an asset for their college-student interns, it will also serve other students in Wayne County, where 50-70 percent qualify for the free/reduced lunch program. Just think: if young people can engage with the environment—our "home"—they will learn how to protect it.

This is where the next work begins, where we rise above the zero point and set anchor. Like the schools we work in, this is where our mission belongs now, in 10 years, in 65. I can't bring Jonny back, but I can set a course for his brothers. Yes, this is where we will leave our mark.

When I walked through the historic Adirondack lodge on the reserve, I noticed an old upright piano sitting in a corner. *There are even possibilities for music here*, I thought. And that's when I remembered: *Nature was his teacher, music was his voice.*

If you know when you have enough,
you are wealthy.
If you carry your intentions to
completion, you are resolute.
If you live a long and creative life,
you will leave an eternal legacy.

—Lao Tzu
Chinese philosopher

Believing Your Work Matters

Mourning takes time.
Knowing if your outreach is effective takes time, as well.

The James McBride Teaching Awards

In 2014, our foundation established the James McBride Teaching Award to recognize excellent teachers serving under-resourced communities and to inspire others to make the same commitment. Through 2018, we've given this award to 28 teachers from various schools, often recommended by their principals.

There are several reasons why we named the award for James McBride. Born in 1957, McBride grew up in Brooklyn's Red Hook projects to become an acclaimed writer and musician. In 2015 President Obama awarded him the National Humanities Medal for humanizing the complexities of discussing race in America.

Jonathan was only 11 when he read McBride's landmark memoir, *The Color of Water*. The book is a tribute to McBride's mother, a Jewish woman from Poland who married into the black community, founded a Baptist church, and put all 12 of her children through college. Jonathan was profoundly moved by the book; it raised his awareness about race and poverty and motivated him to do something.

After Jonny's death I wrote to everyone who had influenced our son, whether they knew him or not. James McBride was one of those people, and he wrote back. As it happens, he lives in our river community and graduated from Oberlin College. James was drawn to our mission to help students growing up in impoverished neighborhoods, as he had. In time he got involved in our programs, starting with a lecture at our summer Jazz Academy. We feel he's a fitting role model for the students we help support.

In October 2008, James agreed to provide the narration for a video we were producing for a World Water Day event. That's when he first told us about the talented students at Creative Arts, the performing arts high school in Camden. To repay James for his time, I bought instruments that the school needed and delivered them to band leader Jamal Dickerson, affectionately called "Mr. D" by his students.

When I arrived at the school, Alex Cummings was there to help me unpack the car. A gifted sax player, he was a senior in Mr. D's class and taking music lessons from McBride. He told me he'd recently been to Boston, where he performed at a high school jazz band competition and also auditioned at Berklee College of Music.

"I think I got in," he said. "But where I really want to go to college is this school in Ohio you've probably never heard of. It's called Oberlin College."

I didn't say a word. Alex kept talking about Oberlin, the school our son would have graduated from if he had lived. To me, it was just another sign: this was where I was supposed to be—here in this old school building, with Alex, carrying secondhand horns and keyboards up to the cramped third floor. I listened to Alex talk about his future, knowing the tremendous odds he had already overcome. I stayed for his music class. And when I left at the end of the day, the sound of girls singing Italian arias followed me down the stairwell. I was so grateful to have discovered such a creative place.

In 2009, we named Alex Cummings our 10th Jonny Scholar. And thanks to Alex's musical prowess, a dedicated teacher, and the persistence of James McBride, Alex became a freshman at Oberlin that September.

TEACHING AS A CALLING

In November 2017, Camden music teacher Jamal Dickerson was front and center on the CBS Evening News. The parent of one of our Jazz Academy students is a CBS cameraman, and he'd successfully pitched a story about Jamal's work at Creative Arts Morgan Village Academy to his news director. I watched the show, thrilled that Jamal's cause was being shared with a wider audience.

"When you go into teaching because you really *want* to, you're more effective," Jamal said. He always says that—for Jamal, teaching is a calling. He's not just a teacher for these kids, he's a role model and father figure. He helps his students see the goodness he sees in them—and by teaching life lessons through music, he helps them see the light at the end of the tunnel.

Jamal grew up in Camden, and knows how unforgiving its streets can be. When we first met, the school was in a rough neighborhood on South Sixth Street. (It's since moved to a newly constructed building in a better part of town.) At the start of his career, Jamal's goal was just to teach his students the E-flat scale and keep them off the streets. Today, after nine years of his teaching, his school jazz band has won so many accolades there isn't enough room to display them all at the new campus in Morgan Village.

It was a joy for me to present Jamal with our James McBride Teaching Award, just months before that CBS film crew showed up. It was a simple ceremony, we gathered around the piano with his eager students. With many role models ahead of them, these students don't just talk about going to college, they *expect* to go to college.

And how do teachers like Jamal turn the odds around? Hard work, long hours and commitment. Let me tell you about some of the other inspiring teachers who've received our James McBride Teaching Award. Their work is all about adapting and finding solutions. So is mine.

Sheria Andrews has many compelling stories about her students in Trenton. At one time she vowed never to return to her home town after college, because she believed the fight was too great. Today she's the Chief Academic Officer at Trenton's successful charter school, Foundation Academies. She tells her students she wants to see them sitting at the table where people make decisions about their community. Sheria understands that she's supposed to be tired as she works relentlessly in this great fight. She is part of the solution.

Lisa Pope was a reporter for the *Trenton Times*. After writing a story on Foundation Academies, she quit her job to become a teacher there. Lisa believes that young people have the power to make a difference, but they don't always believe it. So when her students had to attend school on Martin Luther King Day, even though public schools were closed for the holiday, Lisa taught them a lesson about the inequity in charter school funding. That day the kids took to the streets, chanting all the way to the Trenton State House, where they read speeches they'd written in class. They felt empowered; they felt heard. That's effective teaching.

During a visit to Lisa's classroom, I heard one of her 6th-grade students describe how he had adapted to the demands of his new school. He agreed when I asked if I could include his insight in this book. Despite the mixed metaphors, it aptly sums up how I adapted to grief.

"Handling change is like jumping into a deep river. You better learn to go with the flow or you'll never reach higher ground."
                                    —Kabrien Goss

Our technical world is evolving rapidly. Like many teachers, Jack Lyon, a teacher at AMPS Charter School in Oakland California, teaches his students how to adapt to technology and face the complex changes they will encounter in their future.

Science teacher Mel Fletcher found that the classrooms at Harpswell Coastal Academy in Maine weren't ready for students on the first day back after summer break. So she quickly adapted her curriculum on coastal ecosystems to outdoor experiences, holding her classes at a picnic table and setting up a water-testing lab in the temporary finance office. Without reliable internet or use of a bus, she managed to teach in the natural spaces right in front of her, focusing on what's important to her as a teacher: experiential project-based learning.

Persistent fundraising by Suzette Ortiz's choir at Creative Arts Morgan Village got them to the Show Choir Finals in Nashville in 2015. Though they were one of the smallest choirs participating, they competed in more categories than any other school—and won gold in every one. On the day I recognized Suzette with the McBride award for her 30 years of service, she spoke of the power of music in helping the less fortunate navigate through Camden and beyond.

It's no surprise that in the schools I visit, music is always a big part of the curriculum. Music reinforces life skills. Playing in an orchestra requires a student to negotiate, communicate and collaborate as a team player. Kenneth Woodley, band teacher at North Carolina's Gaston College Prep, said it best on his application for the McBride award. "Music renews the mind and heals the heart. And as a music teacher, I get to set the tone of hope."

In less than a week after that national television broadcast on Jamal, nearly 50,000 people viewed the CBS Facebook post. That segment was all about what I saw in Jamal's band room: possibility.

Some people doubt that urban youth will amount to anything. Not surprisingly, the teachers I meet are most proud of the students who everyone else doubted. They help those kids navigate through unfair situations and offer them fairness in their education. Jill Spiegel, a founding teacher at Foundation Academies, got the Conservatory staff at Oberlin to let her students rehearse on campus, where they made a beautiful recording—yet more proof that kids from "the hood" are capable of real accomplishments.

All these teachers and their students share the same goals, whether their school is on a former peanut farm in rural North Carolina, or in a crumbling brick building next to a crack house in urban New Jersey. Their course is set by hard work and an unwavering faith in the possibilities that lie ahead. They know that stuff is broken all around them, but they remain optimistic. And they are there to witness the times when stuff gets fixed.

At a time when our congressional representatives are dismantling so many supportive community programs, the success of these teachers reassures me that the role we play matters, no matter how small it is. To paraphrase Bonhoeffer, "Nothing can make up for the absence of our son, so we must fill the empty space with our work to preserve the bonds between us."

For our foundation outreach, naming James McBride as a symbol for students growing up in similar circumstances was a no-brainer. It wasn't about our work being effective, but about recognizing the work of others who are.

"Without an education you're a nobody."

—Ruth McBride
Mother of writer James McBride, 1921–2010

MAGICAL THINKING

The Takeaway

I actually believed Jonathan would appear on one of my visits to that wonderfully noisy and disorganized band room in Camden, New Jersey. I needed a sign from him that I was on track with his tribute. A nod or his familiar wink would do.

I know that my search for a sign was crossing the line into magical thinking: I was hoping to make the impossible, well, possible. I have to confess I really thought he would materialize, just like Patrick Swayze did in the movie *Ghost*. On the day I presented our teaching award to Jamal Dickerson, I was waiting for Jonathan to tell me what he thought of the jazz band. In time, the paranormal became normal, at least for me. When the band started to rehearse Ron Carter's "My Romance," Jonathan appeared, grabbed an upright bass and began performing alongside them. And then, just like in the movie, I had a chance to say good-bye to him.

In my magical thinking I forgot the first rule in philanthropy: Nothing we do will ever bring our son back. We can only give his future to others. Effective outreach, for any grieving parent, is about taking nourishment from the simple deed of giving.

CHUKUA

Bob visited Tanzania on assignment in 2010, and that got us involved with the work of Ashley Shuyler and Afric-Aid. Ashley began her outreach there in a classroom too, supporting schools for young African girls. Reading about her transformative experience in Tanzania helped me understand my own role in philanthropy.

I learned the word "chukua," which in the Maasai language means *to give freely*. The English translation is *"take,"* a word the American dictionary has more than 48 definitions for, including acquire, earn, lay hold of, win and make use of. "Take" can also mean to take into one's hands, find out, capture, hire, carry and convey.

But we have no definition for the word "take" that means *to give freely*, to become vulnerable. That's exactly what happens when you step in and give your child's future to others. You become vulnerable. Never forget the second rule of philanthropy: Become vulnerable and take comfort from those who help you heal.

Due to the simple fact that I am still alive, I've been given the gift of time. Time to understand some of the problems facing others and time to support their solutions. I was given time to drive to Camden and deliver a check to Jamal so that every band member could board a downtown bus one minute after midnight and arrive in Dayton, Ohio, by late afternoon for a college admissions audition. I was given time to sit in a hair salon and watch relationships grow between homeless men and women and Trenton students. I heard Julio, a former bass player suffering from cancer, pass on his wisdom about life, gun violence and kindness while he waited for his haircut. The kids will never again look at a homeless person as less than human... and neither will I.

I was given time to become comfortable in tired, uncomfortable places that most people drive around or fly over. I ended up in those places because of Jonathan's death. And remarkably, each place had something to do with music: jazz in Camden, classical in Trenton, rock and roll in the Bronx and a marching band in Gaston. And music had everything to do with my healing. I just listened to Dianne Reeves sing her melancholy interpretation of "How High the Moon". The lyrics express my feelings best when it comes to wishful thinking.

"*Somewhere there's music, it's where you are*
Somewhere there's heaven, how near, how far
The darkest night would shine
    if you would come to me soon
Until you will, how still my heart —
    How high the moon."

Every bit of help I gave also helped me heal. I first noticed how my role in philanthropy changed when we attended the senior concert at Creative Arts in 2009. Matthew and I gave Alex Cummings a new professional alto sax to carry him through his conservatory career at Oberlin. Without missing a beat, Alex clipped his new Yamaha Custom Z to his neck strap and performed "Tribute to Trane," flawlessly. I took in each perfect melodic note he gave back.

That's when the taking started, when the roles reversed. I just knew I was supposed to be there in that auditorium with people who'd never heard of Oberlin College but who would never forget how Alex's performance got him there. Alex gave me hope—and I grabbed it and never let go.

I took from everyone I met. I even took the name they gave me, "Miss Peggy." As my giving was nurtured, I had a sense of belonging, a purpose.

The taking fixed me.

There was no changing fate, and in the end I surrendered to that simple truth. It took me 10 years to scream. Eleven years to surrender. The only way out of my grief was through it.

From grief to generosity. Generosity is what mended me—that, and a bit of magical thinking. It took some time, but in the end Jonny became the inspiration, not the necessity in my grief.

*Nothing that is worth doing
can be achieved in our lifetime;
therefore we must be saved by hope.*

*Nothing which is true or beautiful
or good makes complete sense in any
immediate contest of history;
Therefore we must be saved by faith.*

*Nothing we do, however virtuous,
can be accomplished alone;
Therefore we must be saved by love.*

—Reinhold Niebuhr
American theologian, 1892–1971

AFFIRMATION

On His Way Home

In 2007 we held our son's one-year memorial at Bowman's Hill Wildflower Preserve in New Hope. Friends and family gathered to sing, share remembrances and listen to a short presentation about the initial work of our foundation. It rained, and after the rain let up we walked through the hemlocks in the dark, with only our candles to light the bluebells at our feet. We stopped at a stone bridge that arches over Pidcock Creek, and two guitarists played while we sang a gentle, bittersweet tribute: the Beatles' "In My Life."

One by one we walked past the new cedar bench we'd placed near the water to honor Jonny's memory. The azalea trail beside this winding stream was one of  his favorite routes when he went running in this woodland sanctuary. It was the last place he visited before his fatal drive home.

Four years later, friends were walking the same trail and saw that Jonathan's bench was gone. They called us immediately. After Hurricane Irene hit New Hope in late August 2011, flooding had devastated many parts of Bucks County, including the wildflower preserve. Of the 20 memorial benches in 134-acre Bowman's Hill, Jonny's was the only one uprooted by the storm, even though it had been chained to a landing above the creek.

I felt the same heartbreak as when the police knocked on our door that night five years earlier. The painful memory of Jonathan's last day on earth came back to me. Just as unexpectedly, here was another notification, another loss. Our son was torn from me again.

We realized that the bench was probably lost forever, broken in pieces and, for all we knew, making its way across the Atlantic to the Azores. We were despondent, but having spent five years mourning, we knew how to handle loss. We would just keep working.

And so I traveled with Bob for a job in the Baltics. But a few weeks into the assignment, Bob got a message from a couple who lived a few towns south of us. They told him that after the flood subsided, Jonny's bench had floated up to their dock on the Delaware River, where they dutifully retrieved it.

Turns out they were photo buffs who followed Bob on social media. When they saw our family name on the brass plaque, they contacted him via Facebook.

After Jonathan's bench was knocked off its moorings, it had bobbed along Pidcock Creek, slipped under the county road bridge, passed the historic Thompson Neely House and floated out to the rising, raging Delaware River. I imagined the bench tumbling, sinking and bouncing along the river, following beside River Road, the same road where Jonathan had crashed into a tree on that last day of May.

Finally, the bench landed at a dock about six miles south in Washington Crossing, with only a nick on the right arm to mark its tumultuous journey. Its reckless course was randomly stopped at the property of strangers who just happened to know of my husband. And there the bench stood on their dock, waiting patiently to be reclaimed.

The remarkable journey of Jonny's bench rekindled my faith—this was surely a powerful sign from our son. It wasn't just magical thinking. He was safe; he was saying goodbye.

Call it serendipity, call it fate. All I know is that this incredible thing actually happened.

All of it happened. Raising our child, the sheer disbelief of losing our child, the engrossing journey that followed his death—all this happened. I learned to trust my rise from mourning in places I never would have known.

You don't always need affirmation that you're on track with the work in your child's name. You just have to *believe* that you are.

This evening I sit comfortably on Jonny's weathered bench. As I put my mourning away, I feel nothing but gratitude. I see our beautiful son where the moon and stars slowly fill the night sky. He is quiet. His eyebrow raises; I see him wink. Yes, this *is* heaven, "how near, how far."

Death ended Jonathan's life, but it didn't end his relationship with me.

There is much to be done.

I think of him following the muddy trails in the wildflower preserve and I realize, now, that Jonathan didn't want to be alone.

He was always on his way home.

*The last thing
we learn about ourselves
is our effect.*

—William Boyd
Scottish novelist, 1952–

Resources

BIBLIOGRAPHY

McCracken, Anne and Semel, Mary. *A Broken Heart Still Beats, After Your Child Dies.* Center City, MN: Hazelden, 1998

This is a remarkable collection of literature compiled by a journalist and a social worker who both lost a child. Raymond Carver, Dwight Eisenhower, Robert Frost, Judith Guest, Anne Morrow Lindbergh, Gordon Livingston and William Shakespeare are among the writers whose works explore the death of a child. Their words, seasoned with wisdom and experience, will offer you comfort and insight when you need it most.

Staudacher, Carol. *A Time to Grieve.* New York: Harper Collins, 1994

The author, who recognizes the power of shared experiences in grief, has gathered the meditations of numerous survivors of loss into this powerful book. You can read one page or every page, in any order, and find counsel to heal.

Pallotta, Dan. *Charity Case, How the Nonprofit Community Can Stand Up for Itself and Really Change the World.* San Francisco: Jossey-Bass/Wiley, 2012

   The subtitle says it all. This book will transform the way you think about giving.

Clarke, Cheryl. *Storytelling for Grantseekers, A Guide for Creative Non-Profit Fundraising.* San Francisco: Jossey-Bass/Wiley, 2009

   This is a good, easy-to-read resource for first-time grant writers with a story to tell.

Singer, Peter. *The Life You Can Save.* New York: Random House, 2009

   Australian philosopher recommends charities based on effective altruism. At his website of the same name you can register for a free course on giving well.

Drucker, Peter F. *Managing the Nonprofit Organization: Principles and Practices.* New York: Harper, 1990

   This is the most practical resource on my bookshelf. The thing is, I wasn't ready to read it until I understood where I belonged after our son's death.

Web Resources

These sites proved helpful to us; you might find others that suit your work better.

Nuts & Bolts

Foundation Center: foundationcenter.org

The Chronicle of Philanthropy: Philanthropy.com/resources

Establishing a Nonprofit Organization Tutorial: grantspace.org/ training/self-paced-elearning/ establishing-a-nonprofit-organization-tutorial

GuideStar: guidestar.org

Council on Foundations: www.cof.org/content/ starting-a-foundation

INSPIRATION

Do Something: dosomething.org

Southern Poverty Law Center: splcenter.org

20 Best Nonprofit Websites: topnonprofits.com/lists/
best-nonprofit-websites/

Foundations that honor Sandy Hook victims:
www.courant.com/news/connecticut/hc-news-sandy-
hook-memorial-charities-htmlstory.html

GRIEF COUNSELING

The Compassionate Friends: compassionatefriends.org

The National Center for Grieving Children and Families:
www.dougy.org

Assoc. for Death Education & Counseling: adec.org

Bereaved Parents Help Group: bereavedparentsusa.org

GRATITUDE

IN GRIEF

Our family remains grateful
to everyone who helped us mourn
the loss of our Jonathan.
You brought us casseroles and meaningful books.
You organized his memorial program.
You carried his casket.
You listened.
You let us nap.

IN GENEROSITY

Our thanks to Peter Reiss for creating our Foundation.
Thank you to our friends and family members,
and to all the strangers who responded
to Jonathan's death
by supporting his Foundation.

A special thank you to Jonathan's teachers for encouraging him.

I send a big hug to "Hank" in Ohio
for giving my smile back to me.

I'd like to acknowledge my editor, Barbara Peck,
my book advisor, Andrew Hudson,
and other friends whose words of wisdom guided me
through mourning
and helped me write this book.

and

I remain ever grateful
to
my devoted husband, Bob

About the Author

This is Peggy Oliver Krist's first book. When she couldn't find a handbook to teach her how to create her son's tribute, she wrote it.

Peggy was born and raised in Alameda, California, one of eight siblings. In 1972, after graduating from Whittier College, she headed East to graduate school. Within weeks she met her future husband, Bob, and her life delightfully changed course.

After working as a systems analyst with Volkswagen USA, Peggy spent 30 years as a photo editor and business partner in Bob's international photography career. She managed his stock photo library and publishing company, Old Mill Productions, while raising their three sons, Matthew, Brian and Jonathan.

An inveterate journal keeper, she has been writing since her high school years, but didn't take it seriously until the loss of her youngest son, Jonathan, in 2006. She was inspired to write *Grief to Generosity* and share her family's journey with other bereaved parents.

Today Peggy works with her family on behalf of the Jonathan D. Krist Foundation, based in Bucks County, Pennsylvania, and San Miguel de Allende, Mexico. Her responsibilities include program development, interviewing students and working with motivated people who share the same vision.

About the Foundation

The Jonathan D. Krist Foundation was established in 2006 to honor the memory and charitable deeds of Jonathan David Krist. He was a talented musician, conscientious about his politics and helping the underserved. He loved being outdoors with friends, whether it was jumping into a pile of hay bales or hiking in the wilderness. Jonathan died in a car accident at the age of 19, while a freshman at Oberlin College.

At present, our Foundation partners with two schools in New Jersey to help develop their required music programs. The Foundation awards small community service grants, college scholarships and the James McBride Teaching Award. We support the work of Caminos de Agua, which provides access to clean drinking water for communities at risk in Mexico's Independence Watershed. And through mentoring programs at the Lacawac Sanctuary in Pennsylvania and the Bigelow Lab for Ocean Sciences in Maine, our family is helping to inspire the next generation of scientists and earth stewards.

About Mercy

During our son's wake, someone slipped this passage into my blazer pocket. I still go to it often.

I hope it gives you the same strength it continually gives me.

If you have only one takeaway from my book, let it be this message from Henry Scott Holland. He explores the natural yet contradictory responses to death: the fear of the unexplained and the belief in continuity. This excerpt, taken from a famous sermon Holland delivered in 1910, helps keep my heart and mind together so I can keep doing the work Jonathan didn't finish.

"Death is nothing at all.
I have only slipped away into the next room.
I am I, and you are you.
Whatever we were to each other, we are still.
Call me by old familiar names,
speak to me in the easy way you always used to.
Put no difference into your tone, wear no forced air of sorrow.
Laugh as we always laughed at the little jokes
    we enjoyed together.
Play, smile, think of me, pray for me.
Let my name be spoken without an effort,
without the ghost of a shadow on it.
Life is the same as it ever was.
Why should I be out of mind because I am out of sight?
I am but waiting for you, somewhere very near,
just around the corner."

—Paraphrased from Canon Henry Scott Holland
Professor of Divinity, University of Oxford, 1847–1918

Proceeds from this book benefit
the work of the
Jonathan D. Krist Foundation

jonathankrist.org

CPSIA information can be obtained
at www.ICGtesting.com
Printed in the USA
BVHW030439260419
546487BV00003B/6/P